HEAVEN OUR HOME.

WE HAVE NO SAVIOUR BUT JESUS,

AND

NO HOME BUT HEAVEN.

BY THE AUTHOR OF "MEET FOR HEAVEN."

BOSTON:
ROBERTS BROTHERS, PUBLISHERS;
CHICAGO:
R. R. LANDON, AGENT.
1864.

BOSTON:
STEREOTYPED AND PRINTED BY JOHN WILSON AND SON,
No. 5, Water Street.

PREFACE

TO

THE AMERICAN EDITION.

THE following work by an anonymous author, although but recently published in England, has met with very great favor.

In a note to the edition from which this is reprinted, the author states, "that, within the space of little more than one week, the whole of the first edition of 'Heaven our Home' was sold. Within a few months more, sixty successive editions have been called for. He trusts that this will be taken as an evidence that the views which he has presented of our future home have created some interest in the minds of the reading public."

Since the publication of "Heaven our Home," have appeared "Meet for Heaven," and "Life in Heaven;"

and the united sale of the three works already exceeds one hundred thousand copies. Should this volume meet with similar approval from the American people, the other works will follow in rapid succession.

PREFACE.

I HAVE often felt, that the views which most divines have given of *heaven* are so utterly *negative* in their *nature*, and also so utterly *unsocial* in their *aspect*, that they are more calculated to *repel* the inquiries and longings and aspirations of the children of God after it, than to *allure* their thoughts upwards, and fix their affections and desires upon the things that are above.

The mechanism of our moral nature — God's own workmanship — fits us for a *social heaven*. We are *social beings*. A heaven from which *saint-friendship* and *social intercourse*, among those who are in glory, are excluded, *is* not and *cannot* be a suitable abode for us, who have received from God's own plastic hand those *social affections* which we are to possess for ever. A *social heaven* is, accordingly, the *leading* idea which I have endeavored to embody and illustrate in the following treatise.

Richard Baxter's heaven, depicted in his "Saint's Everlasting Rest," is an eternity of holy repose, free from the sins and troubles of earth. John Howe's heaven, delineated in his "Blessedness of the Righteous," is a calm, intellectual eternity spent in the beatific vision of God. St Paul's heaven is a *being through eternity with Christ*. St. John's heaven, exhibited in the Apocalypse, is a great and gorgeous temple crowded with the worshippers of God. The heaven I have attempted to delineate is a *home, with a great and happy and loving family in it.*

The Bible is the orient sun that has dispelled the long, deep night of darkness that once hung over heaven, and in a great measure concealed it from the view of man. The natural sun, by his rising every morning, brings the earth—our present home—into our view, with its variegated scenery, and its living, busy population. The Bible—God's bright spiritual sun that has risen upon us—also brings by its revelations into our view an eternal heaven, which we who are the children of God are to enter at death, and meet each other again on the other side of the Jordan's floods, and be happy for eternity *there, in our Father's home.*

We *need* a home. What is our life *here?* Look at a river upon earth: you see, in its flowing waters, life's symbol. That river is but a little streamlet in its source, welling out from its small and pebbly fountain: it gradually increases in depth and in width; it never rests; it flows on and on, and still unceasingly onwards, without a moment's pause. So does our life, till at last, like the mighty river nearing the ocean, it flings its waters, with a convulsive and gurgling roll, into the sea that is before the Lord, there to mingle with the living floods of angels and glorified saints, who move and gleam like a great ocean, filling the heavens, and stretching far and wide, and seemingly without a shore. Look at the sun in the sky: you see in it a symbol of life. That sun peeps up into the view of a living world, at his first rising, with but a comparatively dim and feeble shining; he gradually emerges with an increasing lustre from his chamber in the east; he goes forth over us in the sky, like a vessel of light sailing along upon the bosom of the great ocean of space; he reaches his meridian splendor; then he begins to descend gradually towards the western horizon, until at the close of day he passes from our gaze into the expanse beyond, going forth to sail still as a vessel of light over another sea of life in the opposite hemisphere, there to rise and to pour down his beams upon other homes and upon other eyes, but removed from *our* view. It is the same with our life. Our soul is our sun. The thoughts of our minds are the beams of light that gleam forth in their scintillations and radiancy and illumination upon those around us. There is the first glimmering dawn of reason, then the increasing splendor of brightening faculties, then the meridian sunshine of intellectual and moral powers. The zenith of life is reached: our mental sun then begins to descend the western sky of age; the evening of death darkens around; then our soul, if in a state of grace, leaves the sphere in which it moved and shone for a season here, passes over the horizon that bounds eternity and time, the Lord Jesus transferring it to a new firmament, — the hemisphere of glory, — *there* to rise in new splendor before the throne of God; *there* to shine as the brightness of the firmament, and as the stars of God for ever and ever.

It is computed that one of the human family dies every moment. Thus, every tick of the clock, an immortal spirit, as if with the outspread wings of an angel, is flying over the boundary-line of time, and is entering the great world of spirits on the other side.

There is thus a river of living souls continuously flowing from time into eternity. In the bed of that stream, we are all, sooner or later, to take our place, and to pass away; for "as the waters fail from the sea, as the flood decayeth and drieth up, so man lieth down, and riseth not till the heavens be no more: they shall not awake, nor be raised out of their sleep."

How comforting, in these circumstances, is the revelation that God has made to us in his Word,—*we have a home for eternity*, and that *home* is *heaven!*

In the following treatise, I look in upon that home of love. I survey the family assembled there. I view their *intercourse* with each other, and with us who are still upon earth; and I notice the *interest* which they feel in what is occurring here. I also show, that, in the gospel view of heaven which I am led to set forth, death, to believers in Jesus, is *going home.*

It is no cold and uninteresting subject which I am thus led to treat. Was it like music in the ears of the Israelites, whilst journeying in the wilderness, to listen to the accounts, which were orally and through tradition handed down to them, of the land promised to their fathers,—a land flowing with milk and honey, and towards which they were advancing? And will it not be equally comforting to you who are the children of God, nay, will it not be infinitely more so, in the midst of your present wearisome journeyings, to read a gospel description of your Father's home in the heavens, which many of your friends from earth have already entered, where you are again to meet them at your death, when time with you is past, and the world is left?

The descriptions which I have given of heaven have a deep and *personal* interest about them; for heaven is to be *your* home for eternity who read these, if ye are the children of God. The emigrant, who is about to sail to a foreign land, feels that *he* has a *personal* interest in the accounts which he reads about it in the newspapers or otherwise: for he is soon to sail to it, to land upon its shore; and he is to spend there the remainder of his life. The bride, who is about to go to her new home, feels that *she* has a *personal* interest in the descriptions which her friends give her of its site, of its appearance, and of its furnishings; for she has upon her soul the sunshine of the gladdening hope, that she is to spend her future life beneath its roof. *You have a similar interest in heaven.* The sea, the deep-blue sea, is not far off, over the bosom of which you will soon set sail, that ye may land in eternity. The vessel is in the harbor; it is preparing to go forth to plough the bosom of the unseen deep, as Columbus launched forth upon the Atlantic, whilst America, on the other side, was all unseen; the sails are already spread; the pilot is at the helm. You already hear the dash upon the shore, and the roll of the great waters; and soon you, who are believers in Jesus, will be in the position of the emigrant, whilst standing upon the deck of the vessel that is already under sail,—you will look back, and you will look down upon your weeping, bereaved friends, whom you are leaving in your death-chamber; upon your home, with its dark cloud of bereavement lowering around it; and upon the earth itself, receding from your view, and gradually becoming smaller in the distance, till, like the vessel upon the far-off horizon, it flits away entirely from your gaze. You will then rise upwards to heaven, *your home;* you will enter, and join for eternity, God's family *now* assembled *there*. In the anticipation of that abundant entrance into heaven, you can even *now* look up to Jesus upon the throne, and you hear him thus addressing you: "In my Father's house are many mansions: if it were not so, I would have told you. I go to prepare a place for you. And, if I go and prepare a place for you, I will come again, and receive you unto myself; that, where I am, there ye may be also."

CONTENTS.

PART I.

Heaven our Home.

CHAPTER I.

PAGE

HEAVEN A LOCALITY 19

II.

TYPES OF HEAVEN. — EDEN AND CANAAN 38

III.

TYPES OF HEAVEN. — A TEMPLE 44

IV.

TYPES OF HEAVEN. — A CITY 62

V.

TYPES OF HEAVEN. — A HOME 77

VI.

THE FAMILY IN HEAVEN 90

VII.

PAGE

Communion of Saints in Heaven 104

VIII.

Communion of Saints in Heaven (*continued*) . . . 116

IX.

Communion of Saints in Heaven (*continued*) . . . 132

X.

Communion of Saints in Heaven, a Source of Instruction and of Joy 142

PART II.

Recognition of Friends in Heaven.

CHAPTER I.

Recognition of Friends in Heaven 149

II.

Recognition of Friends in Heaven (*continued*) . . 160

III.

Recognition of Friends in Heaven (*continued*) . . 169

IV.

PAGE

Recognition of Friends in Heaven (*continued*) . . 175

V.

Recognition of Friends in Heaven (*continued*) . . 188

VI.

Recognition of Friends in Heaven (*continued*) . . 191

VII.

Objections answered 201

PART III.

The Interest those in Heaven feel in Earth.

CHAPTER I.

The Interest those in Heaven feel in Earth . . 219

II.

Philosophical Evidences for this Interest . . 226

III.

Scriptural Evidence of this Interest 233

IV.

Scriptural Evidence of this Interest (*continued*) . 243

V.

PAGE

EVENTS SHOWING HEAVEN'S INTEREST IN US 253

VI.

EVENTS SHOWING HEAVEN'S INTEREST IN US (*continued*) 268

VII.

EVENTS SHOWING HEAVEN'S INTEREST IN US (*continued* 282

VIII.

EVENTS SHOWING HEAVEN'S INTEREST IN US (*continued*) 295

PART I.

Heaven our Home.

"IN MY FATHER'S HOUSE ARE MANY MANSIONS."

CHAPTER I.

HEAVEN A LOCALITY.

THE subject of the following treatise is one that *ought* to arrest the attention and engage the interest of every member of the human family, and especially of believers in Jesus. Heaven is the locality around which are clustering the highest and the holiest hopes and associations of the people of God. *It is to be their home for ever.* Thus all who are Christians *must* surely feel a holy desire to hear about the dwelling-place in which they are to spend their immortal existence when life with them here is finished, and when, at death, they have bidden adieu for ever to the home in which they *now* dwell.

The exile's heart exults with joy as he peruses a description of the land of his nativity, either in the newspaper or in the more elaborate treatise; for he knows the day is coming when he will set sail for it:

such a description leads him often to look across the deep-blue sea, and longingly and pensively to gaze in the direction where his future home is lying. The pilgrim, in the midst of his desert-journey, opens and reads, with the glowing emotions of a lively interest, the letter which has reached him from his home, and which gives him an account of the dear ones who are there, — his affectionate partner and beloved children, — whom he has the prospect of joining when his journey is finished; and to whom, sitting in the comfortable parlor, he will joyfully recount the incidents that happened to him by the way. The mariner who is afloat upon the bosom of the ocean, and on his voyage homeward, not only consults the compass habitually and carefully, which points out the course in which he is to sail that he may reach the desired and sheltered haven, where he will cast anchor, and be safe and secure, for the billows will then be rolling far away in the distance behind him: he also delights to read the narrative which gives him an account of the country to which he is sailing.

In like manner, *you, who are the children of God*, must feel your hearts' best affections and purest desires enlisted when you think of your eternal home; and you must surely feel *some* interest in an attempt to give you a description of it, what it *is*, and what you are to *experience* when you enter it. This is the task which I now endeavor to execute.

What, then, is heaven? This is no trifling or unimportant question. If I am immortal, and if heaven is to be my home for ever, it is of the utmost importance that I should form a right and scriptural *view* of it. Much of my present happiness will depend upon the particular conception of it which I now imbibe and cherish; and this, again, will exert an influence upon my conduct, leading me to prepare and make ready, that I may enter it at death. Before, however, I proceed to consider *what* heaven is, I will, in this chapter, make a few reflections upon the question, *Where is heaven?*

I believe that the views of many Christians about the "locality" of heaven are quite as indefinite and vague as are the musings of a little child two or three years old respecting the position of India, or of Australia, or of the Cape of Good Hope. With many Christians, all is dark and visionary and dreamy respecting the *fact* that heaven is verily a *locality*, and not merely a *state*.

I believe that the young, generally, have a far more *vivid* though an erroneous view of the exact place *where* the eternal home of the people of God rears its walls than that possessed by those more mature in years. In youth, the heart's affections are warm, curiosity is strong, the imagination is lively; and fancy paints heaven as situated *just above the blue arch of the visible sky*. Ask a child, "*Where* is heaven?" Is there any dimness or doubt existing in the mind whilst giving an answer to your question? No: the finger is instantly lifted up; and, looking and pointing to the overarching sky, the answer is, "*Up there.*"

Advancing years, however, and increasing knowledge, effect a complete revolution in our view of this *locality*. A knowledge of astronomy does this by ennobling and elevating the mind. Astronomy not only exhibits to us the greatness and the splendor of the material universe, but the greatness also and sovereignty of Him who made it; to whom it is a great palace, with its lighted chandeliers burning in every apartment; and through which he walks in his glory and in his majesty.

A similar change of view about the *exact position* of a *departed friend* sometimes comes over our imaginings. Have you not sometimes dreamt, that you saw in the visions of the night some such valued one meeting you in your home, and smiling upon you with the love and friendship which he showed to you whilst he yet lived with you? You awoke in the morning, and saw, amid the light of awakened reason, that you mistook in that dream the dwelling-place of him who stood before you. Would it be right reasoning, in these circumstances, for you thus to conclude: "Because I had a wrong view in the visions of the night respecting the *place* of his present abode, therefore my friend has no habitation at all; or, in other words, has no existence"? It is the same with the *where*abouts of heaven. After the dream of childhood about its localization has vanished amid the descending light of increased knowledge, would it be right in us hastily to jump to the conclusion, "Oh, *heaven is nowhere!* It is not *where* we once *thought* it was, and therefore it has *no existence* at all: it is in *no region* at present"?

Some divines have attempted to get over the difficulty of fixing the present locality of heaven by representing it as a habitation that is not *yet* formed. These theologians place heaven in the same category as the *millennium, the latter-day glory, the judgment-day, the resurrection of the dead;* and, in support of their view, they are in the habit of quoting the following words of the Apostle Peter: "Nevertheless, we, according to His promise, look for new heavens and a new earth, wherein dwelleth righteousness." These words, misinterpreted, have prevented Christians from looking up and abroad upon God's great universe in search of a *local* and *presently-existing* home. Assuredly there *is* a heaven, existing *just now*, into which Jesus, our new-covenant Head, has ascended,—the heavens have received him until the final restitution of all things; where God has established his throne,—a throne of glory that is high and lifted up; in which angels who have kept their first estate have their usual habitation,—"for their angels," says Jesus, "do always behold the face of my Father which is in heaven;" and in which are dwelling "the spirits of the just made perfect;" or otherwise the revelations of the Bible are so many myths. There *is* a heaven, existing *just now:* moreover, it is not merely a *local* but a *material* habitation, into which Enoch and Elijah have ascended, carrying their bodies with them; and into which the resurrection-bodies of all the children of God are to rise after the judgment is over, and where they are to dwell for ever; or otherwise the whole Bible is a novel, and its beatific revelations are merely comfortable dreams.

There *is* a heaven, into which patriarchs have entered who lived long ages near the beginning of the world's history; for they are still alive. At Horeb, God's language to Moses is, "I *am*," not I *was*, "the God of Abraham, of Isaac, and of Jacob." When these words were spoken, the patriarchs had been dead for several hundred years. God asserts they were still alive: he is not the God of the dead, but of the living; for all live to him. There *is* a heaven, into which prophets have ascended, who once acted as the mouth of God upon earth, and made audible in the hearing of the children of men those high and important revelations which the eternal Jehovah for ages sent down from his throne, and from the habitation of his glory, to his children. There *is* a heaven, into which the disciples of our Lord have entered who once followed Jesus in his mission of love in this world, and who still follow the Lamb whithersoever he goeth. There *is* a heaven, into which martyrs have ascended in their chariots of flame, who sealed their testimony to Jesus with their blood. There *is* a heaven, into which believers, from every clime of earth and from every age of this world's history, have ascended; who have been coming from the east and from the west, from the north and from the south, and have been sitting down with Abraham, with Isaac, and with Jacob. From the throne of his love, in these high places, God has been saying to the north, "Give up;" and to the south, "Keep not back: bring my sons from far, and my daughters from the ends of the earth." The redeemed of the Lord have been for thousands of years returning and coming to the heavenly Zion with songs of praise. They are now obtaining, in God's presence above, the joy and gladness that were promised, and sorrow and mourning have for ever fled away from them; and these collected and assembled multitudes *now* stand together in their exaltation, and sing before their God and Saviour the praises of the celestial temple. There *is* a heaven, presently existing, into which ye are to ascend at your death who are the children of God through faith in Christ Jesus.

Where, then, is heaven? The Bible constantly speaks of it as *up*, as *above*. But this language, it is quite evident, is only *relative;* in other words, it merely implies that heaven is away from the earth, and is localized in some distant region of space. The earth, every student of geography knows, is, in form, a sphere, or globe, and has two motions. It has its annual motion along its orbit round the sun: it has also its diurnal motion; or, in other words, it turns completely round upon an imaginary axis every twenty-four hours. Take the case of an individual who speaks about heaven, and who, in faith, looks up to it at twelve o'clock in the day. *Up*, with him, simply means the direction in which he is looking into the great pavilion of space, in a line drawn from the centre of the earth, and the part of its surface upon which he at the moment stands. Let twelve hours pass over that individual's head, whilst meanwhile the earth is revolving in its diurnal motion, and has now brought him into the exactly *opposite* direction, in reference to that great pavilion, from what he was twelve hours before. Let him *now* speak of heaven, and let him look *up* to it, in imagination and in faith: his feet are *now*, in a line leading from the centre of the earth, towards the heaven to which he looked twelve hours before; his head and uplifted eyes are in the entirely opposite direction. Is that man right in his view of the *direction* in which heaven *lies* from him at twelve o'clock in the night? Either there must be two heavens, or all space is heaven; or he is mistaken in his view of the direction in which heaven lies from the earth at one or other of these seasons. Now, because we involuntarily and inadvertently commit this mistake in our view of the situation of heaven,—imagining it localized in one part of space at twelve o'clock in the day, and in the entirely opposite region in space at twelve o'clock in the night,—*is heaven nowhere?* The man would neither be a good mathematician nor a good logician who would draw such a conclusion from the premises.

I believe the Scriptures do not *fix the place:* they *have* not assigned, they *do* not assign, the *exact locality* which heaven occupies in the great pavilion of space, no more than they have fixed definitively the exact locality upon earth *where* Eden was situated. There has been no small controversy among writers on scriptural subjects respecting the site of Eden: one writer has actually placed it in the moon. Suppose I had, in my judgment, fixed upon a particular locality as that of Eden, and had afterwards—either by reasoning, or by observation, or by meeting some one inspired, and getting him to point out to me its exact place and its boundaries—been led to see that I was wrong: does it follow that Eden never had an existence because I was wrong in my *localization* of it?

The Scriptures, I repeat, do not *attempt* to define to us the *exact region* in the great immensity of space *where* heaven is situated. I am not sure, indeed, that they *could* have done this so as to have been understood. Were the earth stationary, and the heavens at rest too, I believe this *could* have been done; but, looking at the earth's revolution round the sun, and looking at the fact, that, for any thing I can tell, the sun may have a similar revolution through space round the outside of the wall of heaven, — which is said to be great and high, and from the radiancy of which the sun *may* derive his light, and thus be a merely reflecting body like the moon, — heaven may thus be in one direction from me at one time, and in the directly opposite at another. Even physically, we speak of the sun being up from us; and nevertheless we are all aware, that, every twelve hours, he is down. An illustration will show the *impossibility* of assigning the exact celestial region. If heaven be stationary, and the sun with his attendant planets, and the stars with their several family orbs, roll in their courses round about it, surveying it like children playing round a fire, its exact position cannot be assigned. Look to that vessel which has cast anchor in the bay, and is at rest at her moorings: it is to be your home whilst you are crossing the Atlantic; but it has not yet set sail. Suppose you go into a boat at a distance of two hundred yards, and row quite round the vessel. Whilst you are making that circuit, in what direction will the vessel be from you? It is quite manifest that it will be at different sections of your circle in entirely opposite directions; and were you to say that the position of the vessel, as seen from your boat, and the direction from which it lies from you, is due west, this, it is evident, would be true only whilst you were at one part of your course.

I cannot tell the exact position of heaven. I cannot stand in the boat — the earth — in which I am now sailing, and point my finger in the exact direction along the ocean of space in which heaven is, — the vessel of glory in which I am, as a child of God, yet to have my home through eternity. But what if heaven, the vessel of immortality, has weighed anchor, and is also under sail as well as the earth? It is manifest, that in this case the difficulty of fixing the situation is greatly increased. The Scriptures have *not* fixed the *locality;* and, as far as I can see, they *could* not do so. But heaven has its *position* in the great ocean of space, just as much as the vessel has that is lying at rest upon the waters, kept there by the anchor.

It may be, that beyond all that is visible, and beyond all that is existing in God's lower creation, there lies and there expands and there gleams beneath the light of God's own manifested presence the heaven of heavens, which forms the *etherealized, luminous, material habitation* in which the children of God are, throughout eternity, to dwell. Heaven may be to the whole material orbs of God's great universe what the sun is to the solar system, — a region of brightness so dazzling, that all the light that is in the universe may be flowing out from it; and thus it may be, that all that is luminous in the lower creation is exactly to heaven what the planets are to the sun, — dark, floating masses, till lighted by its beams.

Do not say, that this view of the situation of heaven removes it to an almost indefinite distance from the earth. Time has, as it were, no *duration* in the reckoning of God. "One day is with the Lord as a thousand years, and a thousand years as one day." Space, upon the same principle, has, as it were, no *extension* in the measurement of God. There is no such thing as *distance*, considered in its relation to him. Space is thus annihilated in God. *Quickness* of transition, to some extent, also annihilates space. The speed of angels may be so great in their transitions from heaven to earth, and from earth back again to heaven, that, far as the regions may be asunder, they may make the passage quick as the gleam of the lightning, and rapid as the twinkling of an eye. The invention of the telegraph has almost annihilated space along the surface of the earth. For any thing I can tell, God may have made known, to those who are above, some nobler space-annihilating invention, through which, though situated on the other side from us of the great pavilion of the universe, they may nevertheless feel that they are at earth's very door. Our thoughts almost annihilate space as they roam to and fro through the great creation, and up and down through the heavens, and round about the throne of God. Angels, glorified spirits, may move through space much quicker than our thoughts do, and therefore quicker than the beams of light move away from the sun into the regions around, and hence so much more quick than the ball when just propelled from the cannon's mouth.

The Temple of Jerusalem was a visible panorama of heaven in its relation to earth. There was the Holy of Holies typifying heaven, whilst the outer courts — where the sacrifices were offered, and incense smoked upon the altar, and the worshippers assembled — represented the earth. A veil was stretched, by God's appointment, so as to conceal the Holy of Holies entirely from the view of those who were worshipping without. So is it with heaven. God has stretched a veil of invisibility betwixt us and his throne, which entirely conceals it from our view. Heaven is, indeed, as much out of my sight, and beyond the reach of my eye, as if it had no existence. The prophet's description of God is, "Thou art verily a God that hidest thyself, O God of Israel, the Saviour." God not only hides himself: he hides also from us the habitation of his holiness. For wise purposes, he holdeth back the face of his throne, and spreadeth his cloud above upon it. For wise purposes, God conceals from us the pavilion of light with which he is inhaloed, as he dwells in the midst thereof; because, whilst we remain upon earth, we are to walk by faith, and not by sight; and because a constant and vivid view of the hosts of heaven, and of the great realities of eternity, would so overpower and paralyze us as to unfit us for the duties of earth and of time. But though God does not show us heaven, does not open to us its regions of bliss, so that they may become visible to our view whilst we remain upon earth, he speaks to us, in his Word, *about* heaven, and tells us, not *where* it is, but *what* it is. A little child is in this country, whose parents are living at Calcutta: that child knows not *where* its parents' home is, nor the *way* to it; but the captain knows who takes that child on board; and angels know *where* heaven is, who will take *you*, believers, home.

Those who are in heaven possess a knowledge of it, independently of the descriptions of the Bible. They see its heights of majesty towering around them; its valleys of joy stretching away in all the luxuriance and fragrance of an eternal summer; its rivers of pleasures rolling through its brightening scenery, and the living streams flowing at their feet, which make glad the city of God. They behold its azure sky arching over them in its meridian splendor, and vouchsafing to them the cloudless expanse of an eternal day, — a splendor of light that never grows dim. There are no stars in the bright firmament that is above them, to dispel, in part, the darkness of night; for there is no night there. Finally, they see the building of God, — the house not made with hands, eternal in the heavens, — the house with many mansions, in which God's great and happy family *meet* and *live* and *walk* and *talk* and *act* and *love.*

Angels have been surveying heaven, and have been contemplating its scenery, for at least near six thousand years; and by their surveys, and flights through the midst of it, they must have now a knowledge of what is to us so mysterious. Abel, the first of the human family who entered there, has been enjoying the vision for nearly six thousand years; and, arrayed in his robes of white, has been walking through it, looking upon its changeless monuments, and exploring wonders that have upon them the impress of eternity. All this is from observation, just as a person travelling through his native land acquires, by viewing it, a knowledge far more accurate than what he received by studying its map or its history. Noah now views heaven from a higher mount than that of Ararat; and how living is the scenery! — *it* is not desolated, as the earth was, by a recently oversweeping deluge. Moses now beholds heaven as he looked from Mount Pisgah upon the Promised Land; but he is not surveying it as a country which he is never to enter: he is already *in* it.

It is different with us who are yet but pilgrims and sojourners upon earth. We have in the Bible the only *inspired* descriptions of heaven which ever will be put into our hands; but these descriptions are not heaven, no more than the pattern of the temple which Moses saw on the mount was the massive and gorgeous fabric reared by Solomon, or than a map is the country it delineates, or a book of geography is the earth, or the plan of a house is the material building, or your portrait is yourself.

With many, heaven is merely a sound. They see the word "heaven" in their Bible; they read about it there: but the great heaven into which Jesus has ascended, where God has his throne, where angels and glorified saints dwell together in love, is *not at all*, or is *but dimly*, realized by them as a *locality*, a *world*, existing entirely apart, and independently of the Bible's descriptions. It is right that such individuals should remember that heaven existed before the Bible was written, and would continue to exist even were there no Bible to tell us what a glorious, holy, and happy place it is. The star that is in the far-distant recess of space, hidden from the view of the bodily eye, exists independently of the telescope that has brought it into view. What does the telescope do to that star? The star is not in the telescope, no more than your friend, whom you see before you, is in your eye. It has an existence independently of the instrument through which you look, and by the aid of which you behold it shining, quiet and beautiful, in its far-distant sphere. The telescope does not *create* the star: it merely *brings* it into your view, and *shows* you *how* — in regions that have never yet been penetrated by the gaze and exploring eye of man, with all his instruments — the heavens are declaring the glory of God, and the firmament is showing forth his handiwork.

In like manner, the Bible does not *create* heaven; but it does to heaven what the telescope does to the most distant star that is invisible to the naked eye, — it *brings* it into view; it *throws* the light of its high revelations over it; it lifts the veil that conceals the great regions of eternal life from our view; and it shows us, in its panoramic delineations, a world existing, peopled by prodigious assemblages, and lighted up with its own peculiar joy.

Heaven is not a state or a character merely. It is quite true, that it is said by our blessed Saviour himself, "The kingdom of heaven is within you:" but, in these words, Jesus is not speaking of the kingdom of *glory;* he is speaking of the kingdom of *grace,* — of the reign of grace in the heart of every believer. It is quite true, that character — a gracious state, the soul transformed into Christ's image by the Holy Spirit — is necessary as a *preparation* for heaven. What would heaven be to you, speaking generally, who have not the *character* that *fits* you for it, were you carried up in your present state of unpreparedness, and set down in the midst of its assemblies, and deep roll of its eternal praises? It would be what the warm, dry beach, on a beautiful summer day, is to the fish that has been dragged up there alive out of the sea, its natural element, and to which the balmy air is quite intolerable; it would be what a beautiful landscape is to a man who is entirely blind; it would be what a delightful concert of music is to a man who is deaf; it would be what a rich and sumptuous feast is to a man who is sick, and who nauseates the taste of the most savory and most delicate food; it would be what the society of the learned and the wise, the noble and refined, is to a man who is profoundly ignorant, whose tastes are depraved, whose habits are such that he feels no pleasure except when in a state of intoxication. *Character* is necessary as a *preparation* for heaven; but what I wish you distinctly to understand is, that character is *not* heaven, no more than your character is your home, — than the qualification fitting you to be one of an assembly is that assembly.

Paul was highly favored in getting a knowledge of heaven in the visions of the Almighty. He was caught up into the third heaven. He looked upon its inhabitants, and listened to the roll of its praises. God, however, conceals heaven from *our* view; but, as I have said, he *speaks* to us about it in his Holy Word. He tells us what it is *like*, and what things upon earth bear a *resemblance* to it. This is the origin of the figures which we find the Holy Spirit in the Scriptures employing to represent heaven to us. These figures are so many lakes, in whose clear bosoms we see the world that is above us reflected. They are so many mirrors, reflecting in their polished surfaces the image of the heaven of heavens. These figures are particularly worthy of notice; for they show that heaven is both a locality and also a place of friendship.

CHAPTER II.

TYPES OF HEAVEN. — EDEN AND CANAAN.

EDEN was a type of heaven; and every reader of the Bible knows that *it* was not only the *home*, for a season, of our first parents, but also a place of *social intercourse*. "To-day shalt thou be with me in paradise." "To him that overcometh will I give to eat of the tree of life, which is in the midst of the paradise of God." What Eden was in its primeval beauty to this world, heaven is to the universe of God. *Heaven is the Eden of creation*, where unfading flowers bloom, and the glow of an eternal summer unchangingly smiles; where trees, whose leaves never wither, impart a cooling shade to those who walk through its bowers; where streams of joy flow everywhere through the valleys, and sparkle and rejoice beneath the beams of an unsetting sun.

Does God walk in Eden with our first parents, and hold sweet intercourse with them? God is doing this to all who are in heaven. He walks with the hosts above through the eternal Eden. He communes lovingly with all its rejoicing inhabitants from off the mercy-seat, and mingles with them in its bowers of bliss.

Did Adam and Eve, previous to their fall, exhibit the bloom and glow and beauty of immortality, and the possession of eternal youth? The inhabitants of heaven stand, in their peculiar beauty as well as in their immortality, before the throne of God. The paleness of decaying health is never seen to overspread their countenances, as they walk through these bowers of paradise. No inhabitant there ever says, "I am sick," or presses a sick-bed, or suffers death, or is ever laid by mourning survivors in a grave. No funeral was ever seen moving slowly and solemnly along the highways of eternal life to the city of the dead, — the lonely churchyard. No bereaved mourner appears in heaven standing sorrowfully at the newly filled-up resting-place, and looking down in tears upon the spot where a once-beloved friend lies. The inhabitants there are in possession of a life without end: they will live as long as God himself, as long as Jesus who is upon the throne, as long as heaven itself will exist; and that will be for ever.

Do our first parents in Eden, as previous to their fall, walk now with God in the light of holiness? *Heaven is creation's Holy of Holies.* It is a holy place, and all are holy who dwell in it. I believe, so bright, so shining, so glorious in holiness, are all the members of God's great family in heaven, that were I taken up at this moment into it, and set down among them, I could no more gaze upon their faces and forms than the Jews could upon the countenance of Moses arrayed in the lustre of God; than his persecutors could upon the face of Stephen, so like that of an angel; than I, with unshrinking eye, could look upon ten thousand suns. Saul was struck blind by the outbursting around his path of Christ's manifested presence. What would I feel were Christ at this moment to unveil himself to my view, surrounded by all these exalted and resplendent hosts? I believe that one look would in a moment strike me blind, and thus spread at once, so far as I was concerned, a mantle of darkness over all the august personages who now move through these peopled heavens.

Do our first parents, as previous to their fall in Eden, dwell together in love? and do they feel their highest and their purest happiness, next to their covenant-communion with God, to spring from their intercourse with each other? Are their bosoms two well-tuned instruments of music, that pour forth their melodious tones in sweetest harmony? Are they as two morning-stars beaming forth in their calm sublimity from the deep-blue azure of a cloudless sky? Are they as two Æolian harps played upon by the same holy gale of love? *Heaven is the paradise of love.* All who are in heaven are living in love. It is the very atmosphere of heaven, — the breath of all its glorious inhabitants, — the language in which they address one another, — the power which lights up the holy eye wherewith they look upon each other. Surely it will be joyful to leave behind us for ever the cruel hatreds of earth, to spend a long eternity in that holy Eden of love, sitting under our Redeemer's shadow, — feeling his fruit to be sweet to our taste, — being led by him into his celestial banqueting-house, — having his banner spread over us for eternity, even the banner of covenanting love!

The earthly Canaan was not merely the *local habitation* of the people of God: it was a place of *social intercourse.* Was Canaan the Land of Promise? Heaven is this to the whole spiritual Israel of God. It is the Promised Land which your God has prepared for you who are believers in Jesus: it is ready for your joyful and triumphant entrance; and when you have crossed the Jordan, and have taken possession, you will live in it, — nay, you will never leave it, — whilst the endless cycles of a glad eternity are rolling over you.

Not merely twelve visitors have left the wilderness of the world to go and spy the Land of Promise, but multitudes, whose numbers cannot be reckoned up, have left the camp of the human family in the world, have crossed the Jordan of death, have entered eternity, and are now in the goodly land. The Holy Spirit is the bunch of grapes which the Lord Jesus has brought out to us from heaven, to give us a foretaste of the fruits which are spread over its vine-clad hills and are enjoyed in its banqueting-houses. Hence says Jesus to his disciples, "I will drink no more of the fruit of the vine with you, until the day that I drink it new with you in my Father's kingdom."

Was the earthly Canaan a land flowing with milk and honey? What is the better land, the heavenly? "The Lamb who is in the midst of the throne," throughout eternity, "shall feed them, and shall lead them unto living fountains of waters; and God shall wipe away all tears from their eyes." They feed upon the fruits of the tree of life; they drink of the rivers of God's pleasures; and thus they hunger no more, neither thirst any more. The Lord God is their sun and shield. They are dwelling in a world of unchanging and of unfailing abundance.

Was the earthly Canaan something like the lighthouse of heavenly knowledge to the world, shining in the midst of an ocean of ignorance, over which a night of deep darkness brooded? Was it Goshen filled with light, whilst a darkness that might be felt was filling the various provinces of Egypt? *Heaven is creation's lighthouse.* It is a world filled with the uncreated light of God's glory, and in which there is no darkness at all. "They who are in it need no candle, neither light of the sun; for the Lord God giveth them light." "There is no night there: the Lamb is the light thereof."

Did the silver trumpet sound every fiftieth year in Palestine, proclaiming liberty to the captives, and the opening of the prison-doors to them who were bound? Was this the joyful experience of the oppressed in Israel when the year of jubilee dawned? "Blessed is the people that know the joyful sound: they shall walk, O Lord! in the light of thy countenance." *Heaven is the world of liberty*: "Jerusalem that is above is free, which is the mother of us all." Those who are in it are free from slavery, from sin, from pain, from sorrow, from death.

CHAPTER III.

TYPES OF HEAVEN. — A TEMPLE.

 *TEMPLE, or church, is a type of heaven:* "Him that overcometh will I make a pillar in the temple of my God, and he shall go no more out; and I will write upon him the name of my God, and the name of the city of my God, which is new Jerusalem, which cometh down out of heaven from my God; and I will write upon him my new name." "What are these which are arrayed in white robes? and whence came they? These are they which came out of great tribulation, and have washed their robes, and made them white in the blood of the Lamb. Therefore are they before the throne of God, and serve him day and night in his temple; and He that sitteth on the throne shall dwell among them."

The great universe is the temple of God's presence. The Church — every believer's soul — is the temple of God's grace. Heaven is the temple of God's glory. A temple is a house consecrated to God, in which he dwells, and meets with his people, and blesses them; and it is a place of *social intercourse*, not only betwixt God and his people who assemble there, but also among these worshippers themselves. The worship of God is the very object for which a temple is built; and the chief purpose for which God reared the heavens and spread them forth was that he might have *one region*, at least, in his vast and boundless dominions, in which the great retinue of followers who are round about him, and the innumerable hosts who are assembled above, might worship him day and night in his temple.

Heaven, I believe, has been too much viewed as a world of mere rest and complete deliverance from all the ills that afflict us here, and too little as a temple; for, if heaven *be* a temple, it is a life spent by us *here* in God's worship, both public and private, through Jesus, that alone fits and prepares us for its holy exercises.

The whole of heaven is one vast temple. The endless eternity above is one continuous and never-ending sabbath.

I cannot tell *exactly* in *what* God's worship in the temple of heaven consists. From various incidental allusions made in the Scriptures, it is evident that *praise* constitutes a *part* of it. I never read of those who are in heaven engaging in prayer to God, as we do upon earth, for the pardon of sin, for the Spirit to sanctify, and for the daily grace which we require. I often read, however, of them engaging in praise. It thus appears that it is Christ alone who prays in heaven and intercedes for us. All the created intelligences who are there spend their glad eternity, not in praying, but in praising.

Do not, however, imagine that the praises of heaven never vary in their subject. You have only to read your Bible carefully to see that there is a very great variety indeed in the subjects which call forth the praises of the assembled hosts who stand before the throne of God. At one time, God is praised by them as the great Creator of all things: "The four and twenty elders fall down before Him that sat on the throne, and worship Him that liveth for ever and ever, and cast their crowns before the throne, saying, Thou art worthy, O Lord, to receive glory and honor and power: for thou has created all things; and for thy pleasure they are, and were created." At another time, for the spread of Christ's kingdom upon earth: "And the seventh angel sounded; and there were great voices in heaven, saying, The kingdoms of this world are become the kingdoms of our Lord and of his Christ, and he shall reign for ever and ever. And the four and twenty elders, which sat before God on their seats, fell upon their faces, and worshipped God, saying,

We give thee thanks, O Lord God Almighty, which art, and wast, and art to come; because thou hast taken to thee thy great power, and hast reigned." The triumph believers obtain through Jesus over Satan is at another time the subject of a distinct song to God by the assemblies of heaven: "And I heard a loud voice saying in heaven, Now is come salvation and strength, and the kingdom of our God, and the power of his Christ; for the accuser of our brethren is cast down, which accused them before our God day and night. And they overcame him by the blood of the Lamb, and by the word of their testimony; and they loved not their lives unto the death. Therefore rejoice, ye heavens, and ye that dwell in them." The conversion of every sinner causes joy to those who are in heaven; and I presume, over every wandered child's return to God upon earth, a special song of praise will be presented to Him who is upon the throne.

The inhabitants of heaven are not spending their eternity in idleness. They feel how much God has done for them; and they show their gratitude to him, for all his great and unspeakable benefits bestowed upon them, by doing his will, by engaging unceasingly in his service, and in the worship of Father, Son, and Holy Ghost. Nor are you to imagine that there is no reciprocation and no mutual and no endearing personal intercourse betwixt the worshipped and the worshippers, — betwixt Him who is upon the throne and those who are assembled before it, — or that the worship consists simply and solely and exclusively of *praise.*

The redeemed from earth have left their Bibles behind them in the world, from whose holy and dearly relished pages they learned God's will whilst here below, and heard God himself speaking to them. Have they no means of obtaining a knowledge of God's mind and will, *now* that they are standing before him unveiled? Being in the presence of a person does not necessarily convey to you a knowledge of his will. So far as I see or can perceive, being in the presence of the eternal God, and at the foot of his august throne, does not necessarily put his children in the possession of Jehovah's will. I believe that the prerogative of seeing and of knowing the thoughts of other beings is possessed by God alone. He only can look into the bosoms of created spirits, and can view what is passing there, even as we look upon a crowd assembled in the market-place, or scan the words in the pages of a book, and in these visible signs see the author's thoughts, and even catch the glow of his sentiments and emotions. I believe that the created inhabitants of heaven cannot look into the bosom of the great God, and see *his* thoughts and behold *his* will, till he gives expression to these in the vocables of heaven, in the utterances of eternity.

Does God, then, make no communication of his

will now to those who are in heaven? Do they nothing but praise, praise, praise? Does God sit upon the throne of his majesty, and does he neither break the silence of eternity, nor make known one new revelation of his will to those who are round about it? If so, then I have only to say, that there is a great difference betwixt God's *present* dealing with those who are in heaven from what it was whilst they *remained* upon earth.

The Scriptures reveal to us the *fact*, that God has been condescending to speak to his people audibly and face to face in almost every age. He spoke thus to our first parents in Eden; to Cain, when reproving him for the murder of his brother; to Noah, in giving intimation of the coming deluge; to the tribes of Israel, when trembling at the foot of Mount Sinai; to Moses, both on the mount and in the tabernacle; to Job, from the careering whirlwind; to the three disciples, upon the Mount of Transfiguration; and to many others, the occasions of which are referred to in the Holy Scriptures. Did God speak thus to none upon earth till the canon of Scripture closed, except to those who are particularly mentioned in the Bible? Has he never spoken to his people upon earth since, either in dreams, in the visions of the night, or in their holy communion with him by day? I am not prepared to answer these questions in the negative. I believe that what God has often thus done to his people upon earth, speaking audibly to them in a language which they understood, and graciously revealing to them his holy will, is just a *glimpse* and *foreshadowing* of what he is doing in heaven; just as his meeting with his people and blessing them whilst here is an earnest and a symbol of what he is doing to his people who are assembled before him above.

A sovereign in his court upon earth is not always silent and uncommunicative to the courtiers and others who meet in his palace. A father does not sit during his whole life entirely silent in the midst of his children and friends. Is not God a sovereign, seated upon his throne, in his own celestial palace? Are not his courtiers and attendants crowding the celestial presence-chamber, and waiting for an audience of the Great King? Is not God a father? and does he not dwell in the midst of his great family, as they wait for the smile of his paternal love, and does he never speak? Does he never look down, either with the condescension of a sovereign or the love of a father? The very *supposition* spreads a gloom and an unsocial coldness over our views of heaven.

I believe, that, whilst the multitudes in heaven are permitted to speak to God, and to hold endearing converse with him in holy and blissful communion,— thus prayer upon earth is a figure of this intercourse enjoyed by the saints,— God condescends to speak to them also upon particular occasions, to break by the voice divine the silence of eternity, and to make known to them both *additional* and *fuller* revelations of his will than they previously possessed.

When a sovereign, upon great occasions, speaks in the palace or in parliament, the assemblies present attentively listen, the hum of their previous conversation is hushed, and all eyes are instantly, in profound earnestness, turned towards the speaker. Oh! then, surely when God speaks from the midst of the light that is inaccessible and full of glory, and from the throne of his sovereignty, and, in accents of divine love, delivers some new and holy communication of his will to the assemblies who are above, the ascending swell and the commingled anthems of praise, that were previously rising from the ranks of angels and of the glorified, will instantly cease and become hushed, like the sudden calm that came down upon the Sea of Galilee, when Jesus rose in the ship, and looked out upon the rolling billows, driven and lashed into foam by the furious winds, and said, "Peace, be still!"

If you ask, "Upon what subjects do I suppose will God speak on these occasions?" I answer, I cannot dogmatically tell; but there are many themes upon which God *may* speak. He may give audible intimation respecting what he wishes angels and glorified saints to do in their several places; he may give information to the whole assemblies above, when another and another of his children press a death-bed upon earth, and single out the angels who are to go down and bear them up in triumph to their rest; he may give intelligence respecting the more prominent events in connection with Christ's kingdom and cause that are taking place in the world below.

Nor may he speak merely about what is taking place in heaven and upon earth: *he may, on particular occasions, refer to the past.* He may describe, in words that are divine, what was taking place throughout his great universe during the long ages that preceded the morning of creation, — *what* he *was* during that period, what he *felt*, and what he was *doing*, and *where* was the shining-forth of his glory; or he may describe the creation of angels, of the heavens, of the earth, of the human family, and of all that exists, and solve, in words conveying a whole flood of light, many of those subjects that have for ages puzzled dogmatizing geologists, and baffled the puny philosophers of earth; or he may refer to the glow of that eternal love in the bosom of Father, Son, and Holy Ghost, that embodied its promptings in the formation of the covenant of grace; or he may assign the precise reason or reasons *why* He who is all power, and all wisdom, and all knowledge, and all goodness, and all love, and who *could* have made his whole universe *a paradise of life, and of holiness, and of happiness,* nevertheless permitted *moral evil* to enter it, to mar, to disfigure, and to spread death over it, — a subject that has been a dark contention both to philosophers and divines in every age; or he may give, in revelations that carry convictions of his equity to every hearer, the *reason* or *reasons why*, in the sovereignty of his justice, he passed fallen angels by, and, in the sovereignty of his grace, made provision for the eternal redemption of fallen man; or he may make known the *solemn fact*, to the entire satisfaction of all, that the incarnation and humiliation and sufferings and death of his only-begotten and well-beloved Son were so absolutely necessary, that there was no *other mode* possible, even to God, to bring salvation to man, consistently with the claims of divine justice, and with the maintenance of the principles of his moral government over the intelligent universe; or he may show the *precise reason* why the *mission* of the Lord Jesus to the world was delayed for so many thousands of years after the *promise* of it had been given to the human family; or he may assign the reason why he did not cause the gospel to be spread through the world instantaneously by a miracle, but left it to be propagated gradually by the living agency of the Church of Christ; or he may tell the listening assemblies *why* it was that he permitted the monstrous systems of religious delusions to originate and exist, that have overspread the world and overshadowed the nations, in different ages, like so many upas-trees; or he may speak of the future, and tell to angels, and to the spirits of the just made perfect, *when* the last day is to dawn upon the earth, *when* the judgment is to sit, *when* the resurrection-morning is to overshadow the world, and *when* the long, dark night of the grave is to roll away for ever.

On other occasions, the Lord Jesus will occupy, if I may use the expression, the pulpit in the heavenly temple. Then, when the Great Preacher himself begins to address the great congregation, the mighty assemblies will instantly cease their song of praise which they are lifting before the throne of God; and, like the rustling foliage of a large forest when suddenly stirred and breathed upon by the passing wind, they will be moved by his holy voice, while, with the eye of their earnest and silent attention fixed upon him, they will listen with a deep and solemn stillness to the words of grace and of love that proceed out of his mouth.

If Christ's eloquence was so sweet and persuasive and fascinating whilst upon earth, that even his enemies were forced to exclaim, "Never man spake like this man," what then is it, what will its power and influence be, whilst heard by the great congregation in heaven?

Do you hesitate to admit the *possibility* of Christ preaching to the assembled hosts above? Notice, in proof of it, these views. Jesus preached whilst down upon the earth here, and prayed, and spoke in the most condescending and familiar manner to his disciples and followers; and he is the same yesterday, to-day, and for ever. "Seeing, then, that we have a great High Priest, that has passed into the heavens, Jesus, the Son of God, let us hold fast our profession." Further, the Lord Jesus is expressly called the minister of the "true tabernacle," — heaven, — of which the tabernacle among the Jews was a mere shadow. "Now, of the things which we have spoken, this is the sum: We have such an High Priest, who is set on the right hand of the throne of the Majesty in the heavens; a minister of the sanctuary and of the true tabernacle, which the Lord pitched, and not man."

The Lord Jesus preached upon earth. His voice was often heard here, making known to those around him the extent and the spirituality of the law of God; the greatness and the fervor of the love existing in the bosom of the Father towards the human family; the movement that had originated in heaven, and that was going forward upon earth, for the salvation of the perishing.

Can it be, Christ's voice is never heard *now* in that heavenly tabernacle where he presides in the midst of his followers? Is Jesus as silent *now* as if he were a statue of white polished marble, erect and motionless, standing cold and still on the right hand of the throne of God? If he mingled with his followers upon earth in all the intimacies of the most condescending and endearing friendship, can it be that he is *now* in a state of isolation and of entire and lonely separation from all the assembled hosts who crowd around him, and who look to him as the great object of their love, with all the ardor and with all the unquenchable glow of that holy feeling? Is that bosom cold *now* in heaven that *once* glowed with such ardor of affection to his people upon earth? Love is not a selfish and silent and an uncommunicative emotion. It *may* be that Christ's voice is not heard alone in heaven as the intercessor of his Church and people, addressing the eternal Father on their behalf. That voice may also be heard addressing angels, and also his people, with an eloquence of which we can form only a very inadequate idea. I may ask, Is the Lord Jesus the minister of heaven? Is he the elder Brother of God's family? Is he the great High Priest who is over the house of the Lord? Do the redeemed follow the Lamb whithersoever he goeth? Does the Lamb in the midst of the throne feed them, and lead them to fountains of living waters? Whilst the Lord Jesus is one with God, is he not also one with the general assembly and church of the first-born? Does he not retain in heaven now the holy social nature which he possessed upon earth? Then rest assured, that Jesus in heaven *mingles* with the hosts who are there, speaks to them, and makes known more fully the unsearchable riches of the love of God. Oh, how lofty and how comforting is the view, that the whole of heaven is a church; that the created hosts who are in it form one great congregation! Jesus is the preacher; and, on these occasions, — you will not, perhaps, call these seasons the sabbaths of eternity; for the whole endless roll of the cycles above is one continuous, holy, calm, and eternal sabbath, — Jesus preaches to the mighty assemblies who are congregated before him, forming a multitude whom no man can number.

There are subjects worthy of such a preacher and of such an audience. On these occasions, Jesus may refer, not in the way of reproach, but as an illustration of the great love wherewith he has loved the children of men, to the *unspeakable sacrifices* which he made to bring them salvation; how he spent his past eternity, before the world was, in holy love, and in holy communion and in blissful fellowship with the Father and with the Spirit, and, in the fulness of time, left it; how he had glory with the Father before this world was, and, in the day of his coming to earth, veiled it for a season; how He who was in the form of God, and thought it not robbery to be equal with God, nevertheless made himself of no reputation, and took upon him the form of a servant, and was made in the likeness of men; how He who had been throughout a past eternity the Father's delight, rejoicing always before him, became a man of sorrows, and acquainted with grief; how He who was the mighty God, the everlasting Father, became a Child born and a Son given upon earth.

Jesus may also describe the wonder and amazement and intense thrill of awe that spread through heaven when its onlooking assemblies saw a new and mysterious eclipse beginning to come over Him who is the Sun of righteousness, and the veil of concealment commencing to hide the shining-forth of his divine attributes.

It is true, the Scriptures do not reveal to us what new emotions, what wonder, what feelings of amazement, were circulating through the bosoms of those in heaven when they beheld the Son of God leaving the throne. But is there no new sensation in a home when a beloved son is preparing to go out from it upon some important mission? Is there no sympathetic emotion in a kingdom when a beloved monarch leaves his throne, and lays aside his royal apparel, and forsakes his palace and his courtiers, and goes forth upon some important emprise of difficulty and of danger? Nay, is there no tumultuating sorrow in your hearts who are parents, and in the bosoms of the other members of your family, when you look upon a beloved child going out from you, amid the solemnities of the funeral day, to be laid in the grave? Jesus may represent to those who were not *then* in heaven the emotions that thrilled through it when the fulness of time dawned; when he bowed the heavens, and came down. He may describe too, more particularly than the *Scriptures* have done, the depth and the terribleness of his sorrow, which he endured for the salvation of the lost; how he trod the wine-press alone, while of the people there was none with him; how he felt in the garden of Gethsemane, when "his soul was exceeding sorrowful, even unto death, and his sweat was as it were great drops of blood falling down upon the ground;" how he felt upon the cross, when the Father withdrew from him the light of his countenance, the sensible tokens of his love, and when, in the horrors of deep darkness and desertion, he exclaimed, "My God, my God, why hast thou forsaken me?" how the darkness that came down upon the earth was the shadow of the deeper darkness that was upon his soul; how he felt when sleeping among the dead; how he felt when the resurrection-morning dawned, and when the angel from heaven was in the act of rolling back the stone from the door of the sepulchre, and when he was rising the conqueror of death; how the heavens were moved when his ascension from the Mount of Olives, and from the midst of his assembled followers, was taking place, when the everlasting doors were lifted up, and the gates of glory were flung wide open, that, amid thousands and tens of thousands of attending angels, he might return to his native heavens; how the thrill of an indescribable joy shot through the bosoms of all who were in heaven, when they looked up, and saw him seated in his glory upon the throne with God. What communications may not Jesus thus make to the listening assemblies, whilst the joyful cycles of a long eternity are rolling on! What new revelations of God, of himself, of the Holy Spirit, of the ways of God with man, may not Jesus thus make!

So, too, Jesus may describe to the assemblies the various events that are taking place upon earth in connection with his kingdom, — the name of every new penitent, the spread of his cause among the nations of the world. When not engaged in making known to the great congregation views such as I have suggested, will he not condescendingly walk with his followers in heaven, and talk with them personally in the language of eternity? He did these whilst upon earth. Is he not acting similarly towards his people who are now with him? Joyous indeed will eternity be that is spent in this holy and personal and loving communion.

I address myself to you who are the ambassadors of Christ, the heralds of the cross, the messengers of peace to men from Him who is King in Zion. When you take your position in the pulpit on the holy sabbath of the Lord, and stand up in the name of a reconciled God, a risen Saviour, a Spirit who is love, to preach to your fellow-worshippers the gospel of Christ, and to ask them to behold the Lamb of God who taketh away the sin of the world, remember whose representatives you are. Whilst you are addressing the listening assembly before you, elevate your thoughts and views, and remember that you are doing in the sanctuary upon earth what Jesus *may* be doing, and probably *is* doing, in the temple of heaven. Look up in faith to Him who is your new-covenant Head; preach with the same glow of holy affection, with the same tenderness and sympathy and love of souls warming your hearts, that are now pervading the bosom of Jesus.

CHAPTER IV.

TYPES OF HEAVEN. — A CITY.

CITY is a type of heaven; not in its morality, but in the *concourse* of its citizens, and in their *intercourse* with each other. By far the most splendid description of heaven which the Bible contains is given by the Apostle John in the twenty-first chapter of the Book of Revelation: "And I John saw the holy city, new Jerusalem, coming down from God out of heaven, prepared as a bride adorned for her husband. And I heard a great voice out of heaven, saying, Behold, the tabernacle of God is with men, and he will dwell with them, and they shall be his people; and God himself shall be with them, and be their God. And God shall wipe away all tears from their eyes; and there shall be no more death, neither sorrow nor crying, neither shall there be any more pain: for the former things are passed away. . . . And there came unto me one of the seven angels which had the seven vials full of the seven last plagues, and talked with me, saying, Come hither, I will show thee the bride, the Lamb's wife. And he carried me away in the spirit to a great and high mountain, and showed me that great city, the holy Jerusalem, descending out of heaven from God." Surely we may well say, "Glorious things are spoken of thee, O city of God!"

The new Jerusalem hath a wall of glory great and high, fifteen hundred miles in height, according to the measure of the angel. It has twelve gates, and at these gates twelve angels are standing with unslumbering eyes. They are looking forth, as you look forth from your home with watchful anxiety when you are expecting a beloved one's return, upon the nations of earth, and upon the homes of the human family scattered over the surface of the world below them; and they are welcoming into heaven the pilgrims of time who fall asleep in Jesus, and who are going up to the city which hath foundations, as a cloud, and as the doves to their windows. The gates of the city are twelve stones most precious; the streets of it are pure gold, in brilliancy and purity like to transparent glass. The heavenly city is not lighted with lamps at regular distances burning along its streets: it hath no need of the sun, neither of the moon, to shine in it; for the glory of the Lord doth lighten it, and the Lamb is the light thereof. The nations, the multitudes who are saved, are walking in the light of it, and are rejoicing in the splendors of a day to which no night comes. The gates of heaven are never shut; and angels are bringing the glory and honor of the nations into it.

Angels bear Elijah up into heaven, when, in the form of horses of fire and of a chariot of fire, they rise with him in the whirlwind. Angels carry Lazarus up from the rich man's gate, and place him, as the nurse places the child in its mother's arms, in Abraham's bosom. Angels are around Jesus at his ascension in countless multitudes, whilst upon the bosom of a cloud he returns to the bosom of the Father. And these angels at the gates of the holy Jerusalem welcome their companions in who bear home to the city of God the spirits of the just made perfect, — those who wash their robes, and who make them white in the blood of the Lamb.

When heaven is called a city, the figure reminds us that it is a place of *concourse*, in which many are assembled. London is a large and crowded city. Vast multitudes dwell in it, and throng its bustling streets: but, in the *number* of its citizens, it is no more to be compared to heaven than one solitary grain of sand lying by itself upon the washed rock of the beach is to be compared to the beds of sand that lie along all the seashores of earth; or than one ray of light is to be compared with the whole encircling ocean of sunbeams that stream forth from the sun in every direction, and penetrate far and wide into the great pavilion of space; or than one drop of dew that hangs upon the point of the bending grass-blade, and shines in the morning light, is to be compared with the waters of the earth.

Who can take the census of the angelic hosts that move to and fro through these golden streets? "The chariots of God are twenty thousand, even thousands of angels." "I beheld, and I heard the voice of many angels round about the throne and the beasts and the elders; and the number of them was ten thousand times ten thousand, and thousands of thousands."

Who can number the spirits of the just made perfect, the general assembly of the church of the first-born, who are met in heaven? "It became Him, for whom are all things and by whom are all things, in bringing many sons unto glory, to make the Captain of their salvation perfect through sufferings." "After this I beheld, and, lo, a great multitude, which no man could number, of all nations and kindreds and people and tongues, stood before the throne and before the Lamb, clothed with white robes, and palms in their hands; and cried with a loud voice, saying, Salvation to our God which sitteth upon the throne, and unto the Lamb."

FAITH'S VIEW OF HEAVEN FROM THE MOUNT OF GLORY.

The angel takes the Apostle John to a mount of glory, rearing its lofty summits to the east of the new Jerusalem, and commanding a full view of the holy city, spread in its vastness and glory and populousness, as it were, at his very feet. Place yourself, in imagination, upon the top of that mountain, beside the Apostle John and his angel-companion, and with them look down upon the city of the great king; and, lo, you see that it is not only a place of *concourse*, but of sweet and endearing *intercourse*. There is the clear serene, without a vapor; above and around, one unsetting sun; for the Lord God is heaven's sun. No cloud ever sails across to darken that firmament. The air is peaceful; or, if it move at all, it is like the gentle breathing of an infant when asleep upon its mother's breast. The joyous calm of heaven's eternal sabbath spreads its pure and holy peace over its whole population. And there is the celestial city itself, extending far and wide, its twelve gates standing continually open, through which the weary pilgrims from earth pour incessantly into the metropolis of the universe; at these gates, twelve angels, whose faces are turned towards the highways by which the children of God come home to the realms of rest, intent upon the same object that moved Lot at the gate of Sodom, when, evening after evening, he watched the approach of strangers, that he might give them the welcome and the shelter of his home. "Who is this that cometh up from the wilderness leaning upon her beloved?" Far beneath in the distance, and emerging from the clouds of earth and the mists of time, there appear guides, encircling, in her upward flight, one of the daughters of God's spiritual Israel, who has just died, whose ransomed spirit has even now struggled free from its connection with the motionless body. She has left a home of sorrow, where a great change has just taken place. A bereaved partner is standing in it, gazing, with a heart like to break, upon the changed countenance of her who was previously so dear and so lovely in his eyes. A new-born child is lying asleep, and all unconscious that its mother has left it, so that it never can enjoy a mother's care. That child of God, freed from the trammels of the body, parted from those she loved so tenderly, and surrounded by her companions, rises higher and higher, approaches nearer and still nearer to the city of the living God. There is a cry of many commingled voices rising from these angels who form her bridal train, and are conveying that beloved one, who has long been betrothed to Christ, up into the holy city, where dwells her beloved. "Lift up your heads, O ye gates! even lift them up, ye everlasting doors." Lo, the angel at the gate towards which these rejoicing guides are approaching goes forth to meet that child of God, and to welcome her into the city of habitations.

Yonder, also, you observe the patriarchs walking stately and slow among the other citizens of the new Jerusalem. You can distinguish them by their dignified and majestic mien, as they move among their younger brethren. These lived long ages in the world below, whilst the earth was yet young: they seemed, whilst there, to be in possession of something like an endless and unchanging existence. They were the oaks of earth among its fading flowers. They have lived long ages since they rose, and became the citizens of heaven; and they are yet, as they ever will be, in the freshness of youth.

You behold also, not far off, another company, with countenances more pensive and studious, their eyes piercing, but calm, as if meditating upon subjects that waft their thoughts far away from the scenery around them. These *are the prophets of the Lord of hosts.* The descending irradiations of prophecy from the Spirit of the Lord once shone upon their souls, and illuminated the beclouded evolutions of the dark future. They were gifted with a faculty, whilst down upon the earth, which God did not bestow upon other men, — the faculty of looking forward, and beholding events that had not emerged and risen and made their appearance upon the surface of the great onflowing river of Time. They looked not back like the historian, as he reviews and chronicles the events of the bygone; they looked not around upon society to form portrait characters: their eyes were fixed steadfastly upon the regions before them; those realms, over which, to the eyes of other men, impenetrable clouds rested, — the darkness of a starless night. The habits of mind which these children of God contracted upon earth have been carried up with them to heaven. *Grace is just glory in the bud.* These prophets of the Lord still gaze with the eye of a calm and earnest penetration upon what is to occur in the regions of bliss. Yea, the book they read, and which they keep incessantly spread out before them, is the book of eternity.

Turn your eye towards the throne of God. You see an amphitheatre, its crescent of rainbow hues stretching in front more than half way round about the throne of God and of the Lamb. There are seats of honor placed there, each glittering in the uncreated light of God's presence, as if formed separately of the precious stones, multiplied twelvefold, which constitute the gates. Seated upon these are twenty-four apparently honored citizens, with crowns of glory on their heads, and arrayed in robes of white. What *are* they? Are they virgins dressed for a marriage-party? and are they seated there awaiting the approach of the bride, that they may form in the bridal train, and become her bride's-maids at the altar? No: they neither marry nor are given in marriage in heaven. Are they so many children in their innocence, and dressed in their robes of white for the baptismal font, and about to be given up by their parents in covenant to God, to be baptized by the high priest? No: baptism is an ordinance that does not exist here. Are they new-come saints from earth, who have lately entered heaven, and are waiting that they may be crowned by the Captain of their salvation, before all the assembled hosts, with the crown of glory that fadeth not away? No: they are crowned already. Upon twelve of these seats of honor are enthroned the twelve apostles of our Lord. They spent a life of toil upon earth. They resembled, whilst down in the world below, the four living creatures that you see above them, who are full of eyes before and behind, and who rest not day nor night, crying, "Holy, holy, holy is the Lord of hosts: the whole earth is full of his glory." These disciples left their homes and their friends and their native land in the cause of Christ. They faced cheerfully persecution and fire and sword, and even death itself, whilst carrying the banner of the cross in their zealous hands to the ends of the earth. But they went undismayed as the ambassadors of Christ, for it was the King of Zion and the Head of the Church sent them forth; and they perambulated the world as the messengers of the gospel of peace, bringing to those who were afar off from God the overtures of reconciliation. As the heralds of the cross, they everywhere proclaimed that God in Christ was, in covenant, reconciled, and was stretching forth the sceptre of mercy to every member of the human family; "waiting to be gracious; not willing that any should perish, but that all should turn to him, and live." Each of them breathed forth these words of ardent longing in the execution of their evangelical mission: "For Zion's sake will I not hold my peace, and for Jerusalem's sake I will not rest, until the righteousness thereof go forth as brightness, and the salvation thereof as a lamp that burneth." How much did they endure! and now you see what has followed as their reward. They gave forth the laws of heaven, for the regulation of the conduct of men, whilst they remained upon earth; and now they interpret, for the guidance of the citizens, the will of Jehovah for ever. On the other twelve seats are enthroned the twelve patriarchs, in solemn and august majesty, as if they were the elders of the celestial Church.

You may observe, also, a large company, arrayed, like the others, in white, and whose countenances seem as if mantled with something approaching either to the lingering remains of former sorrow that has not quite passed away, or to the remembrance of an anxiety which has followed them up even to rest. They are like ships which have suffered by fire at sea, but have managed to reach the harbor, where they have got repaired and improved, but yet exhibiting the lingering traces of former disaster. They are at rest, like weary and lately benighted pilgrims who have finished a long journey, and have reached their home with difficulty. Now peacefully reposing under the altar, the concave of heaven is ringing with their full-toned and melodious praises; and yet they appear to have upon their faces the shadow of disappointment seated in the midst of joy, a dimness resting upon the face of transparency, the few spots that appear upon the face of the sun, a thin, fleecy cloud floating upon the clear-blue sky; and consistent with these manifestations is the song which they raise: "How long, O Lord, holy and true, dost thou not judge and avenge our blood on them that dwell on the earth?" *These are the holy martyrs*, who sacrificed their lives for Christ's kingdom and crown. They sealed their testimony with their blood, for they loved not their lives unto the death; and over them the heavens are called to rejoice. The gate through which these now exalted and gladdened ones left the world, with all the transactions of time, and entered into that pavilion of glory where they now sit, and where they now enjoy freedom from pain, and exemption from fire and sword and wild beasts and the torture of man, was a gate of blood and of pain. Through much tribulation they entered the kingdom. "What are these which are arrayed in white robes? and whence came they? These are they which came out of great tribulation, and have washed their robes, and made them white in the blood of the Lamb.

Therefore are they before the throne of God, and serve him day and night in his temple; and He that sitteth on the throne shall dwell among them." How joyful and ecstatic must the rest of heaven be to these, when they compare it with what they endured when their bodies were literally roasting in the flames, or quivering under the tooth and claw of ferocious animals, or scalded to death in the boiling caldron, or choked in the stagnant pond or running stream!

The chair in the pilgrim's home is comfortable and soft, when he enters and sits down upon it, after the toils of his fatiguing and exhausting journey are over. The calm of the haven is refreshing to the mariner, when in full sail he enters it, and casts anchor there in safety, and leaves far behind him the storm and the hidden coral reef, the mountainous waves and the terrible breakers: so must the rest and peace of heaven have been sweet and overjoying to these holy martyrs, when they rose from their mangled and bleeding bodies, and entered upon the enjoyment of God's love to them, by the efficacy of Christ's blood, through which alone they have obtained pardon and eternal salvation.

But look yet again. There, too, on Mount Sion, towering in its grandeur almost to a level with the mount upon which we stand, are assembled multitudes, so young and so fair in their appearance. You know who gave this inspired description of them: "And I looked, and, lo, a Lamb stood on the Mount Sion, and with him an hundred forty and four thousand, having his Father's name written in their foreheads. And I heard a voice from heaven, as the voice of many waters, and as the voice of a great thunder; and I heard the voice of harpers harping with their harps; and they sung as it were a new song before the throne, and before the four beasts and the elders; and no man could learn that song but the hundred and forty and four thousand which were .redeemed from the earth. These are they which were not defiled with women; for they are virgins. These are they which follow the Lamb whithersoever he goeth. These were redeemed from among men, being the first-fruits unto God and to the Lamb. And in their mouth was found no guile; for they are without fault before the throne of God. And I saw another angel fly in the midst of heaven, having the everlasting gospel to preach unto them that dwell on the earth, and to every nation and kindred and tongue and people." These are those who died in the world whilst they were yet young. Over them, Jesus said to their parents, when reluctant to give them up, "Suffer little children to come unto me; for of such is the kingdom of heaven." Now they are with Jesus. With *them*, the less of earth, the more of heaven; the briefer life, the earlier immortality. How joyful and comforting would a look upon these beloved ones be to many a poor sorrowing mother still upon earth! — the child of her affections, whom she saw sicken and die, like a flower in the bud destroyed by the early frost, now happy among these immortal companions!

But let your eye wander searchingly over these crowded streets, and try to single out and individualize those happy citizens in their uniform robes of glory. There cannot but be upon some countenance, among all these that are looking up to you, the smile and recognition of former friendship. Near to the fountain of life there is a once dear and tender mother. How different that glorified being from that which I looked upon lying cold and ghastly in her home of sorrow! The Jordan of death is rolling its dark and deep swellings far away in the distance from her now; and with what ecstasy I meet again the smile of that countenance which was once to me as the light of the morning! By her side are friends talking with her in the language of heaven,—a sister, who left us in the dawn of life, and forsook *our* home upon earth to enter *this* home of love; another is a father, who left us in more mature years to enter this glad heaven; and *now* these saints of the Most High, who were lovely in their lives, whom death parted for a season, have met in this world of life, never to be parted again.

There are others among the fair citizens, other members of our family, who are there in the great world; and others, also, who were once my companions and neighbors and friends. Farewell all, for a season, beloved ones! My time is not yet come, but soon my God will call me home. Then I will rise from my bed of death, where I will, I hope, fall asleep in Jesus, as you have done before me, and then join you for eternity in this peopled heaven of yours. I will then dwell with you for ever beneath the overshadowing of God's presence; walk with you under the light of yon great Sun that never sets; and talk with you in your own language about the glories and the joys of the new Jerusalem, and the past scenes and associations and recollections of earth.

CHAPTER V.

TYPES OF HEAVEN. — A HOME.

OF all the types through which the Holy Spirit speaks to us in the Holy Scriptures *about* heaven, there is not *one* that exhibits it in such an endearing aspect, and which instantaneously awakens in our souls such a flood of tender and of hallowed associations, going so warmly and touchingly at once to our heart, as when he tells us, not merely once, but in many a varied description, that heaven is a *home*, in which there is assembled already a *great* and *glorious* and *happy family*, and in which we, who are the children of God, are to spend with them innumerable ages.

It is not *one* type alone, but the *various figures* of the Scriptures *combined*, that give us the truest view of heaven. This is the reason that has led me to dwell for a little, as I have done, upon the earthly similitudes,—*Eden*, *Canaan*, *a temple*, *a city*. I now proceed to a more particular consideration of the type, *heaven our home.*

Those who are in heaven are often spoken of in the Scriptures as constituting but *one family;* and, in all such passages, it is *implied* that heaven is a home. The house in which the members of a family live and associate, whether the palace, the hall, or the cottage, is their home. Heaven, again, is expressly called *the "house of God," "our Father's house."* A child's father's house is its home. *Our* Father's house is to be *our* eternal home who are the children of God. "We have a building of God, an house not made with hands, eternal in the heavens." "In my Father's house are many mansions: if it were not so, I would have told you. I go to prepare a place for you. And, if I go and prepare a place for you, I will come again, and receive you unto myself; that where I am, there ye may be also." "Surely, goodness and mercy shall follow me all the days of my life; and I will dwell in the house of the Lord for ever."

The great universe is the *house* of God, — which he more than fills; for he made it, and the Creator must be greater than the creature, — in which he walks in his majesty to and fro, and in every part of which he manifests, by the works of his hands and the evolutions of his providence, his awful presence. The earth, the Church, every believer's soul, is the house of God, in which he now reigns in grace and through grace. Heaven is the home of the sanctified, where his scattered children are all at last to meet, and in which they are to dwell together in love for ever.

The word "home" awakens in the bosom of every individual many tender and hallowed and dearly-loved associations. You, to whom I now speak through these pages, may not be at home just now. You may be a sailor, in the midst of strangers, and tossed far away upon the rolling billows; or you may be a soldier, bivouacking in an enemy's country, and exposed to all the perils and deprivations and fatigues of war; or you may be a traveller, at a great distance from that home which is so dear to your soul: but you *have* a home awaiting your return in your native land. Your parents are there, and often speak about you to their friends and neighbors, and take a pleasure in showing the letters to them that you statedly send. Or if they are both dead, and are sleeping together in the family grave, and there be no dwelling *now* upon earth to which you can give the name, "my home," *you had a home once.* In the days of your youth, you lived with your parents there; shared the smile of your mother; partook of the kind attentions of your father; and played, a light-hearted and reckless boy, or romped, a warm-hearted girl, with your brothers and sisters. The word "home" has with you around it *now* the tender and hallowed and never-to-be-forgotten associations of the *past;* and to you surely the announcement must be a comforting one, that you *have* a home still, if a believer in Jesus; and that *home* is *heaven*.

Do I address myself to some of you who are parents, watching with affectionate care over your children, who are growing up before you in wisdom and in stature, and with increasing love to God, to each other, and to you? You are looking hopefully upon their minds becoming brighter and brighter in the knowledge and in the ways of God, like the morning light, the increasing splendor of the rising sun. You are contemplating with emotions of pleasure their quiet, kindly, loving walk with each other in the journey of life, and feel your heart glad at witnessing the reciprocation of these amiable feelings. Surely, whilst in the midst of such enjoyment, and whilst watching hopefully over your immortal charge, you must feel a comfort in the thought, that, if believers in Christ Jesus, you the parents and your dear children will yet constitute a portion of God's great family; for you have a home of love that is already prepared for you. Death will part you sooner or later; but you can even now say to your children, in the anticipation of leaving them, and of entering heaven before them, what Jesus said to his sorrowing disciples, "I will see you again," up in our Father's home, "and your heart shall rejoice."

Or it may be that you are brothers and sisters, dwelling together in love, and experiencing, under the smile of your heavenly Father, the outgoings of the dawn and the twilight rejoicing over you. With glad and lightsome hearts, you lie down at night under the guardianship and watchful eye of the great Shepherd of Israel, and rise in the morning, and take your seat day after day at the family table, enjoying the affectionate care, the heavenly conversation, and the holy example, of your parents. You feel that your present home is every thing to you. It is Eden, with its sunshine, and its roses clustering around the door, and hanging in graceful tendrils from every window; its birds of song upon the wing, carolling so gladsomely over your heads. It is a bower of bliss in the midst of a desert of sorrow; the retreat of all that makes life happy; where Love has set up her throne, and reigns supremely over all the social and Christian affections of your souls. It is the sheltered tranquillity of the haven, where the sailor upon the voyage of life casts anchor, and feels secure from the rolling billows and the fearful hurricanes that are raging in their fury on the outside and far away in the distance. It is Noah's ark of peace and protection to the dove in the midst of the world's encircling deluge. You feel secure in the inside; for the Lord in love has shut the door, and you are under his covenant protection, whilst the great world around is the wide waste of cold waters. Your home is, in this case, the *image*, the *symbol*, the *panorama*, of heaven.

Or it may be that you are confined to your sick-chamber, and are now laid down upon your bed of death. Your head is pressing in much pain your uneasy pillow; your heart and flesh are beginning to faint and to fail; you feel that you have not long to live; your friends are gathered around your dying bed, looking upon you with that earnest, shrinking glance, and with that distressing gaze, which give evidence, that, in their opinion, you will soon, very soon, bid them adieu. The rising sun is just beginning to pour his brightening beams into your sorrowful dwelling, shadowing forth to your friends around you the morning of a glorious eternity, that is bursting out with its flood of light upon your waning eye. You shake hands with your weeping relatives, who are at your bedside, like an individual setting out upon a long journey, or embarking in an emigrant vessel; and you bid them an affectionate farewell. You have taken the last look of the home you are about to leave, and of the well-known, dear, but sorrowful faces that are around you; your spirit is struggling to be free; angels are hovering over you in their sympathy and love, waiting till the last spasm with you is over, that they may conduct you in triumph to the realms of life, to the brightness of eternal day. Is your name enrolled in the Book of Life? Are you a child of God? *How comforting to you, in your present circumstances, is the knowledge that heaven is your home!* Death to you will thus merely take you out of *one* home, that it may usher you into *another*. You can leave and go out from your weeping friends with the full and gladdening assurance, that you are not departing to be a homeless wanderer for eternity. Your disembodied and living spirit is not to traverse for ever the wide and boundless universe of God in search of a home, and find it all dark and empty and unpeopled, and discover no refuge for eternity in any part of it that will open its friendly door and admit you to its rest. *You have a home for eternity in heaven;* and, at the very moment of your dissolution, you can look up in joyful hope, and exultingly exclaim, "For I am now ready to be offered, and the time of my departure is at hand. I have fought a good fight; I have finished my course; I have kept the faith: henceforth there is laid up for me a crown of righteousness, which the Lord, the righteous Judge, shall give me at that day; and not to me only, but unto all them also that love his appearing." Nay, more: death is thus to you not simply a passage out of *one* home, that you may rise and enter *another:* it is a passage from the midst of the warm, loving bosoms of the present members of your family, who are dear to you, up into heaven, to become associated for eternity with the warmer and more loving bosoms of God's great family, who are waiting for you to join their happy number with songs of unspeakable joy.

Again: a home is the abode of love, or rather *should* be so; the place of union and of peace and of holy brotherhood. In this it is the very *image* of heaven. Around the very *word* "home" what holy and sacred associations cluster and hang! what young, joyous, and refreshing thoughts! what hallowed imaginings! What soul-gladdening, cherished remembrances hover around that word! In what heart does it not awaken these emotions? Yes: it does this even in the hearts of those who have disgraced their home by their misconduct. Amid their scenes of vice and of misery, they have fond recollections of it; even as our first parents still had loving and holy associations hovering around Eden, after being driven out of it.

We have not far to look for some young woman, who, like a withered flower, rudely plucked by the hand of the seducer from the stem upon which it had bloomed, is now heartlessly flung out of her domestic bower, a scandal to Christianity, a disgrace to her sex, and the source of misery and wretchedness to herself and to others. She is wandering among strangers, far from her parents' home, dwelling now in the haunts of sin; but, oh! even yet, the *holy remembrances* of the not far-distant past, like the lightning at night, bringing the dark thunder-clouds more frowningly into view, flicker across the darkness of her present sinful path, and fill her bosom with feelings and emotions of the bitterest remorse. Reflection sleeps, it is true, and is too often drowned in the laugh of her guilty companions who are around her, in the hilarity of the licentious song, in the cup of intoxication which she now presses to her lips. Memory, however, *sometimes*, in an hour of calm reflection, brings back, flashing full upon her view, the scenes of innocency, of love, of holiness, and of joy, that were around her in her girlhood, but which have passed away from her like her days of former purity. These reflections leave her heart lone and desolated, torn, bleeding, and dark. And what is her history? That young woman, who now walks with an apparently unblushing brow in the paths of sin, was once a virtuous, timid, and shrinking creature, the prayerfully-tended opening rose of her parents' home. The morning dew of her innocent youth sparkled upon the leaves, and made her shine in all the beauties of at least an external morality and an outward purity. She grew up from infancy to girlhood, gradually expanded in her beauty, and passed at last into the full bloom of womanhood, "with the rose upon her cheek and the lily upon her brow, and the fragrance of the hawthorn in her breath, and the blended light of heaven in her smile; the idol of her mother, and the pride of her father."

The old story: A young man in the neighborhood, attracted by her beauty, began to pay to her his addresses, with apparently honorable intentions. Their acquaintanceship ripened into friendship, their friendship into love, on her part; on his, into something else. Visit after visit, that *pretended* lover endeavored to undermine her principles of virtue by speaking to her about how other young women had acted previous to their marriage with their present husbands; and he succeeded in producing in her bosom a feeling of decreasing horror at the thought of sin; and he led her, step by step, to assume a hollow trust and a false confidence in him, by telling her that he would save both her feelings and her character by an honorable marriage, — a promise he never meant to fulfil. That young man — who has a mother, too, and she is of the same sex as his victim — cruelly, heartlessly, diabolically *seduced* at last, in an unthinking and thoughtless and terrible hour, that fair and credulous girl; and, oh, the bitter fruit of sin! In an agony of shame and remorse, she slips, with her heart like to break, away from her parents' presence, and from the hallowed precincts of her youthful, perhaps rural, home; and now she has become, in the crowded city, a withered leaf, tossed upon the ocean of crime. Ah! as that now ruined and miserable creature creeps into her wretched dwelling, — which is not her home; she is there merely as a lodger, retained for the horrid gains of iniquity she brings to the owner, — she feels that that retreat of degradation and shame is not her home: the peace and the joys of home never visit her there. Go to her, even in that place. Be an ambassador of Christ to her. Speak to her, in the words of love and of earnest entreaty, about the ruin she has brought upon herself, and about the shame and pain which her conduct has flung upon her distressed and sorrowing parents, upon her blushing sisters and affronted brothers, who mourn over her in their home of sorrow, and still see what she was once in every rose that blows during the summer in their little cottage garden, and hear the music of her voice, during her youth, in the song of the lark that sings so sweetly in the sky above them in their sorrow, and who are longing for, and yet fearing, her return. Tell her that she *has* a *home* still; that her mother and father are in it; that they still have warm hearts beating glowingly towards her, and that they would receive their poor ruined and wretched daughter. At the mention of the word "home," you might see how her dim and callous eye kindles and flashes; how her face, sad with the clouds of sorrow upon it, brightens up; how her heart heaves, and she bursts into tears. Yes, that word "home" has a charm which softens even the hardest heart, revives holy associations, and awakens a longing desire to return to it in the bosom of the very guiltiest wanderer.

What effect, then, should be produced upon you, who have wandered from God in a life of ungodliness and guilt, by the assurance that in him you have a Father who is looking down upon you in love, waiting to be gracious, beckoning you to return, and telling you that in heaven you have a *home*, the door of which is ever standing open for you to enter? Do you not feel, at the thought of that home which God has provided for you, that in your life of grace, and preparation for eternity, you have something worth *living for*, nay, something worth *dying for?*

Take another picture. A young man is about to be married to one who has long been the object of his affections; who, with a warm, confiding, and virtuous heart, reciprocates his love. He has already prepared the home, to which, with his attending friends, he is about to conduct his blushing bride, — as Adam conducted Eve to the nuptial bower, when he received her in all her beauty and innocence from the hand of the Lord, — where, for the remainder of his life, he is to live with her, and where he will feel in her presence a new sun risen in the firmament of his happiness. That home which he is soon to enter in these circumstances, and in which he is to spend life with her who is all fair in his eyes, and every way worthy of his love, is every thing to him; and he longs to be there.

Such is your position who are believers in Jesus, and the children of the living God. Christ, your beloved, the spiritual bridegroom of your souls, has gone up into yon glorious eternity that is above you. He is even now preparing and making ready heaven for you, to be your home of rest and joy for ever, in which you will spend a glad and an endless eternity. You are now looking up with this longing desire for an entrance into yon home. "I have a desire to depart, and to be with Christ, which is far better." And that longing will soon receive a glad and eternal realization. The day of the solemnization of your spiritual espousals with Jesus is drawing near. Then He who is "fairer than the children of men, the chiefest among ten thousand, and altogether lovely," will come forth at your death to take you up, escorted by a great company of attending angels, that where he is, there ye may be also. You can even now look up to heaven with the same feeling that enlivens the bride as she looks to her new home, to which she is soon to be conveyed: it is your future and eternal mansion of love.

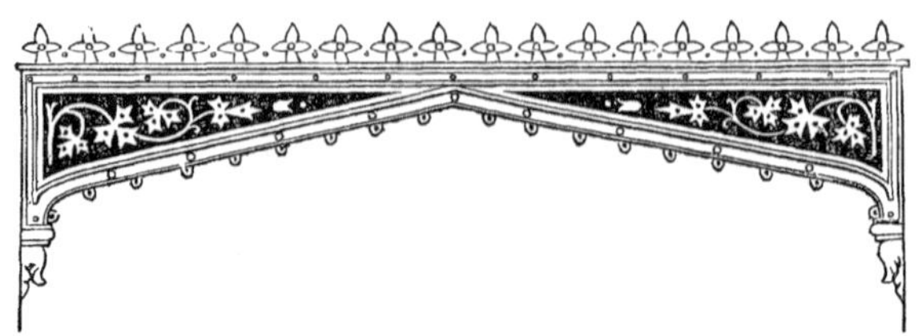

CHAPTER VI.

THE FAMILY IN HEAVEN.

HEAVEN is not a home—empty, deserted, and lonely—like what many of the homes around us in the world become through the influences of time and of disease. "Time does not breathe on its fadeless bloom:" there is in it "no more death, neither sorrow nor crying, neither shall there be any more pain; for the former things are passed away."

A glorious family is already met there, where a Father is presiding in love. There is upon his countenance neither the scowl of the despot nor the frown of the cold and unfeeling judge. The smile upon his countenance bears evidence that he is not a severe and exacting master merely, but the Father of mercies, and the God of all comfort. There is the love of a Father in his look as he turns his eye downwards, and condescendingly listens to the song which the countless assemblies present to him, as with one heart and one voice they proclaim, "Salvation to our God which sitteth upon the throne, and unto the Lamb." There is the benignity of a Father upon his brow as he contemplates his great family rejoicing round about him, and feeling in their bosoms the flowing tides, the ever-running streams, of an exceedingly great joy; the affection of a Father in his bosom, that ever glows with benevolence towards all the members of his family; the welcome of a Father in the outstretched arms of his endearment, whilst he beckons his children to approach him, that they may speak to him individually, and hold personal converse with him, as a loving child upon earth does with an affectionate parent in their home of love. There is the emotional tenderness and the love-tones of a Father in his voice, whilst conversing personally with all who stand round about the throne of his sovereignty.

The Lord Jesus is upon the throne with God, the brightness of the Father's glory, and the express image of his person. He is the *elder Brother* of heaven's great family. As the souls of the just made perfect reflect the image of Jesus, Jesus himself reflects the image of the great Father of lights. He is not there lifted high and apart, and far removed from the feelings and sympathies that are pervading the bosoms of those who are round the throne: he is, on the contrary, mingling with them in the utmost condescension and fraternity and holy familiarity. He is acting towards all his brethren in the heavens the part of an attentive and affectionate elder brother towards a younger sister; watching over them in love, taking them by the right hand, bearing them upon his arm. He is feeding them, and leading them to living fountains of waters, wiping away all tears from their eyes.

The Holy Spirit is the fountain of life, and is the source of undying love, — the wellspring of immortal joys in the bosom of every member of the great family. He is the Breath from the four winds of heaven, descending in living currents upon all its inhabitants, enabling them, with the full and ever-gushing aspirations of gladdened hearts, to pour forth, to Father, Son, and Holy Ghost, their anthems of adoration and praise. He is the Fire from off heaven's high and holy altar, which glows so intensely and so unquenchably in the bosom of every child of God.

Angels compose a *part* of that great family. I cannot tell their number; nor do I believe their number *could* be set before the human family in the arithmetic of earth. I cannot describe their glory nor portray their beauty. The splendor of Gabriel's countenance was so great, that, when the Prophet Daniel — a man greatly beloved — looked upon it, he could not stand upright, and gaze, but fell with his face upon the ground. The angel that came down from heaven to roll away the stone from the door of Christ's sepulchre is thus described: "His countenance was like lightning, and his raiment white as snow." The angel who appeared to the shepherds by night upon the plains of Bethlehem, to announce the advent of Jesus to earth, was so shining, that his presence filled the plains with light. In this splendor and beauty of countenance and form, the whole angels of heaven — God's first-born children — stand and sing before the throne of God, and give glory to *Him* who *was*, and who *is*, and who *is to come*. I cannot tell whether angels, who are the morning-stars of eternity and the sons of God, differ in the traits of their features, and the glow of their countenances, as females do. When a painter wishes to draw the portrait of an angel, he forms the image of a beautiful woman, and then simply adds to her a pair of wings. This shows his inability to comprehend an angel's beauty. The Bible does not describe whether there exist these differences. We must enter heaven before we can know. But I can learn from the Bible, that angels differ in rank in the scale of dignity and honor which God has appointed them to occupy in heaven; for, besides the angels, there is the archangel, also principalities, powers, cherubim, seraphim. We never read of angels feeling envy towards those who are in a higher position in the scale of promotion; and they mingle familiarly with the saints.

The redeemed who have returned and come to the heavenly Zion — the whole glorified members of the human race — compose *another portion* of the family now assembled in heaven as their home of love. I have already referred to the *fact*, that the number of the redeemed must be very great; so great, that they are beyond calculation. That this may be easily conceived, we have only to remember what is the number of believers in a home compared with the children of God who live in all the different places of a parish; what is the number in a parish compared to those living in all the different parishes of Scotland; and, by thus continuing our comparison, we come to the contrast between the number who are living at *present* in the world and *all* the children of God who have lived and died, and gone up into heaven, during the near six thousand years which have rolled over the world.

I cannot describe in adequate language the appearance of these redeemed ones. We must be contented with the consideration, that they now bear the image of Jesus, whilst he is the image of the invisible God, the perfection of beauty: which is more than the concentration of all that is fair in this world; for far short are the things of earth compared with those of heaven.

Angels who have kept their first estate, the redeemed who have come out of every nation and kindred and people and tongue, and have met together, make up the family of God; and they constitute but *one* family. They are watched over and loved by the same Father. They are ministered to and guided and instructed by the same Saviour, their Lord and Master, their new-covenant Head, the universally Beloved of them all. They are gladdened and refreshed by the life-giving breathings, by the sweet and comforting influences, of the same Holy Spirit. They are the happy inmates of the *same home* of love. They walk together through the garden of the Lord, or sit together in its roseate bowers. They travel, in larger or smaller groups, the valleys that are stretching around. They sing, as the united and affectionate members of the same family, heaven's song of praise. Their voices rise and mingle in one harmonious stream of melody to Him who is upon the throne. *Heaven,* in short, *is their home;* and it is a habitation of peace and love.

Again: as, in the members of a family upon earth, there is a *family likeness*, apparent in the midst of *peculiar* and *individualizing traits*, of features, complexion, and form; so is there a *family likeness* existing among all the members of the family of God, both in heaven and upon earth. *Love* to God, to Jesus, to the Holy Spirit, and to all the members, is one feature. I address myself to you who are the children of God by profession, and followers of the Lord Jesus. Have you, I ask, *this feature* in your moral image? *Do you love God?* Have you the love of God shed abroad in your hearts by the Holy Ghost which is given unto you? Were Jesus at this moment to speak to you from the throne of heaven, to break the silence of eternity, and to put the question to you which he once did to the Apostle Peter, "Lovest thou me?" could you look up to him whose eyes are as a flame of fire; who searches Jerusalem even as with lighted candles; who penetrates the hearts, and who tries the reins of the children of men? and could you say, "Lord, thou knowest all things; thou knowest that I love thee"? Do you love the Holy Spirit, who has kindled his own love-breathings in your soul, as one fire kindles another, or as one candle lights another? Allow me, then, to ask you this question: How does the love of God in your soul manifest its presence? Is it a mere kindly, inactive, and inoperative glow, only showing itself in words, and never flowing forth in a stream of warm, active, beneficent deeds?

You may come to be able to answer by studying the nature of some earthly love; say, of one of Eve's daughters, who responds to your affection, and from whose eyes come those demonstrations of pure feeling which fall warm and glowing upon your heart. You will quickly perceive that your affection to her is an active principle, and instinctively leading you to love all connected with her. You love the home where she dwells; and, some way or another, you never feel happier than when your footsteps are upon the path that leads you to it. You love her parents, who with fond parental affection are watching over her. You love the brothers and sisters who smile upon her. You love to be in their company, even when she is not present; for they speak to you about her: their very voices are pleasant to you, because they sound, not so musical and sweet, but something like hers. The letter which she has written with her own hand, and which she has sent to you, describing, with a shrinking and timid caution, the feelings of esteem she bears towards you, has a charm in it. The shady walk, along which she wanders alone, and reads apart from the world the letters you send her, giving full expression to the warmth of your honorable affection, carries the same secret virtue. Above all, you love to be in her company, to see her smile, to hear her voice, and to feel your heart delighted in the sunshine of her presence.

Have you this evidence that the love of God is in your bosom, — that you possess this trait of the family likeness of God's children? Do you not only love God, but all connected with him? *Do you love the Lord's Day?* During its hallowed calm, when the din of labor is hushed, and you are set free from the distractions, pursuits, and pleasures of earth, — during the sabbath's sweet and hallowed hours, do you feel upon your spirit a holy calm and a peaceful elevation, as if heaven was descending upon you with its ineffable rest, and its fervor of kindling and intense desire after God? Whilst its holy and peaceful hours are passing over you, are they to you a foretaste of those joys that are at God's right hand, and of those pleasures that shall endure for evermore?

Do you love the Lord's house, and long to be in the church, that you may meet with Jesus there, sit under his shadow, listen to his voice speaking to you in that of his ministering servant — the man of God who occupies the pulpit — who is an ambassador for Christ to you, and in his name beseeches you to be reconciled to God? Whilst wending your way peacefully and meditatively towards the gates of Zion, do not these words give expression to your holy, heavenly, breathing desires? — "How amiable are thy tabernacles, O Lord of hosts! My soul longeth, yea, even fainteth, for the courts of the Lord; my heart and my flesh crieth out for the living God." "Oh, send out thy light and thy truth: let them lead me; let them bring me unto thy holy hill and to thy tabernacles. Then will I go unto the altar of God, unto God my exceeding joy; yea, upon the harp will I praise thee, O God, my God. Why art thou cast down, O my soul? and why art thou disquieted within me? Hope in God; for I shall yet praise him, who is the health of my countenance and my God." Oh, yes! it is necessary that you experience the same glow of affection, the same elevation of thought and of contemplation, the same kindling warmth and celestial fervor, the same buoyancy and alacrity and exultation of spirit, whilst joining God's worship in his house of prayer, that his glorified children feel in heaven, when their voices rise and commingle and swell upwards and upwards in the temple of glory above. This fervor and joy in God's worship is a distinguishing feature in the family likeness of all his children.

Do you love the Lord's Word? Do you love it because it is the gift of God to you, the revelation of his holy will as David did, who thus speaks of it?—"Oh, how love I thy law! it is my meditation all the day." "Thy word is very pure; therefore thy servant loveth it;" "sweeter also than honey and the honeycomb." Do you read the Bible with the same feelings of kindling delight, and with the same awakening associations of pleasure, with which the lover reads over and over the letter which he receives from the mistress of his heart? And do you go to the Bible daily as the hungry man repairs to his meal, as the weary and thirsty traveller turns aside to the spring of cooling and refreshing waters which he meets at the side of his path? Is God's Word your salvation, your desire, the man of your counsel, the guide of your life? Do you follow its leadings as the Israelites in the wilderness followed the pillar of cloud by day and the pillar of fire by night, that you may learn from it the path in which you are to walk that you may reach your Father's home? Do you keep your eye upon the Bible with the same anxiety and care that the mariner looks upon the pointings of his compass, whilst afloat upon the bosom of the ocean? It appears that even God's children in heaven delight to observe God's Word: "And I John saw these things, and heard them; and, when I had heard and seen, I fell down to worship before the feet of the angel which showed me these things. Then saith he unto me, See thou do it not; for I am thy fellow-servant, and of thy brethren the prophets, and of them which keep the sayings of this book: worship God." This clinging of the soul to Holy Writ, and holy longing after its sweet and heavenly revelations, is another trait in the family likeness of God's children, both in heaven and upon earth. It is to be hoped you possess this feature of the child of God; that you feel a holy delight whilst listening to the tones of your heavenly Father's voice speaking to you in its inspired vocables, and whilst perusing its high and heavenly revelations.

Do you love the Lord's people, — all who bear the image of Jesus, whose life is hid with Christ in God? If you have love for the father of a little child, you love that child for its father's sake. This sympathy of love is a universal law, not confined to man, but extending to the higher creation. So should you love, then, the children of God for *their* Father's sake. This love to the brethren is the very foundation of what is termed *the communion of saints.*

Attraction exists among all material bodies,—the communion of saints among all the children of God. There exists among all *material bodies* the *principle* of *attraction:* so, too, there exists among all the children of God—if not counteracted and neutralized by sin—a breathing, longing desire after fellowship and communion with each other. *This communion of saints* is not confined to the children of God upon earth: it exists also among those who are home in heaven, who are standing before the throne of God, who see each other's countenances in the light of a glorious eternity, and who speak to each other in the language that God's children use in heaven.

What is implied in the *communion of saints,* as it exists among the members of God's family? If you look at the intercourse which the members of an affectionate family enjoy with each other in their parents' home, you will see in *it* the *symbol* and *visible representation* of the *intercourse* and *fellowship* that are even *now* existing among the members of God's household.

Happily, we have all experiences of home,—the continuous affection of the members to each other, their converse, the nameless little attentions which affection prompts them to perform, all independent of the mercenary motive of obtaining a reward. The history of a family is a history of our affections: how these are gratified by the quiet walk in each other's company; the talk about the heavens declaring the glory of God, and the firmament showing forth his handiwork; how full the earth is of God's goodness; how they are naturally led to look up in hope, and to think and speak about heaven as their eternal home, where their heavenly Father is waiting to receive them; how they are to meet when the journey of life with each of them is finished upon earth; and how they are to spend their eternity in their heavenly Father's home of love. Then, where there is a separation during the day or for a longer period, how fondly you find the members, when they meet again, speaking to each other about the past, and about all that has happened to them in the providence of God since they parted!

This, I believe, is taking place among the members of God's great family in the heavens. They dwell together in their Father's home. They speak with each other in the language of heaven. Their communion and fellowship is with God, and with his Son Jesus Christ. They have intercourse also with each other. They have their fellowship-walks of holy friendship, during which they will speak to each other of all God's dealings with them in preparing them for home; will naturally refer to the past journey of life, and to what happened to them by the way along which their heavenly Father led them, and at last conferred upon them the unspeakable blessing of meeting, and living together for ever.

Perhaps the telescope, upon earth, is a mere *approximation* to the *power of vision* which God's glorified children possess. They may scan the heavens, and gaze not merely upon what is existing before them and around them, but look also everywhere onwards upon the great universe, and talk together of what they see; and who shall try to follow that vision, even in imagination? This will lead them to speak with each other, not merely about the evolutions of God's providence in the *past*, but also about all that they behold going on around them, both in heaven and throughout the boundless universe of God.

CHAPTER VII.

COMMUNION OF SAINTS IN HEAVEN.

IT has often occurred to me that we might particularize these fellowships and conversations in heaven, not only without being exposed to the charge of presumption, but with manifest advantage. Image, then, with me, my reader, yon venerable-looking pair at the very verge of the valley which stretches far away in its verdant beauty, and is bounded by a pure river, whose waters are flowing as smoothly, fully, and calmly as if Peace herself had there established her reign. They are walking alone, and loitering, with placid contemplation, among gorgeous amaranths. These are Adam and Eve. They have been long in heaven, long associated there, not as husband and wife, — many of the relationships that existed upon earth are not needed in heaven, and thus no longer exist there, — but in the higher and holier affinities of that love and praise enjoyed by the angels. They have long held sweet intercourse together. For more than five thousand years, they have walked to and fro among its gardens and palaces; but do not suppose that their vision is yet blunted, their hearts weary, or their affections waned. Among other subjects, they are doubtless speaking about the terrible loss which they and the whole of their posterity sustained through the fall, and how much they were to blame for the guilt of that *black act.* They are talking about the cunning of the old Serpent when he planned the temptation for Eve, and the wily way in which he made his approaches along the avenues that led to the citadel of a holy and unsuspicious heart. They are discoursing of the great mystery of redeeming love,—how God, who brings light out of darkness, order out of confusion, and life out of death, so overruled, in wisdom and in love, their fall, as to give through it the human family to occupy a higher place in the scale of existence than they enjoyed before; for he gave up his only-begotten and well-beloved Son, to *assume*, and thus to *exalt*, the nature of fallen humanity: so that man, who was made a little *lower* than the angels, is actually, through the fall, *raised* above them, and placed upon the right hand of the throne, in the person of Jesus.

The subject leads them to the success of Christ's great undertaking, the while they are gazing around them upon the numberless assemblies of their posterity. In these great crowds, they have the evidence that their Redeemer's death has not been in vain; for they are, with gladdened eyes and rejoicing hearts, looking upon the millions of millions who have been saved by the blood of Christ, and been ushered into heaven to praise him there for their salvation. The expression of delight upon the countenances of these our first parents is proof that they feel no ordinary emotion of gratitude to God, whilst they hold this sweet intercourse in the fellowship of heaven, and speak of the fallen race; for, far as their joyful eye can reach, they see their children's children, even one hundred and sixty generations, at last rejoicing before them,—a great revenue of souls gathered by Christ into the exchequer of heaven.

Realizing still further this view, you may hear these two venerable fountains, from which the great stream of the human family is still flowing, and will continue to flow till the river is lost in the ocean of glory, giving expression to two anxious wishes. The first is, that their posterity who are yet upon earth could see the great and eternal reward which God has provided in the heavens for all who believe in Jesus upon earth; that the inhabitants of the world might thus be led to live under the influence of these great realities, and under the powers of the world to come; that, whilst *in* the world, they would live *above* it, and make their whole life upon earth a season of earnest and unwearied preparation for the world above. The second, that the glorious gospel of the blessed Jesus were spread in its light and liberty and power over the whole earth, and that the Sun of righteousness were risen upon all the dark and benighted lands of heathenism that are still the habitations of cruelty and superstition. Nor is it possible but that Adam and Eve must look down from their seats in the skies, and walks of bliss, upon these nations of earth, in their sin and degradation, with the same feeling that pious and affectionate parents look upon their once-innocent children, now become the inmates of a prison, or the occupants of still more infamous abodes.

Image again, and picture, those two seemingly much-attached saints, arrayed in white, with crowns upon their heads, and sitting in that recess where never-fading flowers cluster so thickly over it and around it as to form a holy retreat, and scene of seclusion. There, where love breathes over the scene, and has established a throne in each of their hearts, they discourse of the past, and chiefly of the leading events of their lives previous to the time when they rose at their death, and met each other for eternity. These are Jacob and Rachel. First as cousins, in the endearments of a holy friendship, and then in the nearer and dearer relationship of husband and wife, they were lovely in their lives, whilst down in their home upon earth. So, in their eternity, they are not divided. They have met in heaven, and have met never to part again. They are sitting far retired from the congregated assemblies, and are engaged, it may be, in such discourse as this.

Jacob's mind is upon the past, whilst he says, "O Rachel! the ways of God with his people in the world are truly wonderful, and often mysterious. Yea, when I look back upon my own earthly life, I see in its varying events a vivid manifestation, that, whilst the Lord reigns in love, his way with his people is often in the sea, his footsteps in the deep waters, and his paths not known. How hoveringly do clouds and darkness hang over and around his dealings with his chosen! Do I not recollect with what anguish of heart I left my dearly-beloved mother, Rebekah? and how the frequently mysterious and dark dispensations of his providence led us, and brought us at last to meet in this world of eternal love? I did what was wrong in stealing my brother's birthright, and in deceiving my father by telling him the lie. God punished me for my sin by stirring up against me the wrath of my justly offended brother. By my mother's advice, I left the home of my youth to go to your father's for a season, until my brother's wrath should pass away. I acted upon my mother's counsel, and left my parents. I did so with a heavy heart and sorrowful spirit. I had merely my staff in my hand. It was on a bright summer's morning I left, before my brother Esau had risen, and whilst my father was yet asleep. The birds were singing over my head as gladly and cheerily as yonder myriads are now praising God. The sun was risen, and was looking out upon our home as joyful and glad as if he did not see one sorrowful heart. The streams were playing on in their courses, and glittering beneath the beams of the morning sun, utterly unmindful of our sorrow, and the lambs were gambolling round about us, when my mother came with me a short distance out from our dwelling, shook me by the hand, and, bursting into tears, commended me to the keeping and guidance of my covenant God, the great Shepherd of Israel, whose eye slumbers not nor sleeps. Every thing around me and my weeping mother was glad, and exulting in the sunshine of the morning; but our poor hearts were sorrowful and sad at the thought of separation. I shook hands with her, turned from her in tears, and entered upon the desolate path that was to lead me onwards towards your father's. I reached Bethel just as the sun was going down. I felt exhausted and tired. I took some of the stones, and placed thereon my weary head, without any fear at the loneliness of my situation: for I knew that God was everywhere present; that he would encircle me in his covenant embrace, watch over me in love, defend me from all harm. I fell into a sweet sleep, during which I had a heavenly vision,—a ladder not far from me, standing upon the earth, with its top reaching to heaven. I saw the angels of God. I recognized those who were my visitors there, very soon after I entered into heaven, ascending and descending upon it. I saw the vision of the Almighty, and heard the voice of the great God speaking to me out of this very heaven in which we are now met, and giving me the covenant promise of the land upon which I was lying, and intimating to me that my posterity was to be very great. In the morning, I rose, and left that place with the commingled feelings of gladness and of holy awe. Pursuing the path that led me to your father's, I remember well how my heart danced with joy when I first saw you, and met you at the well; for you were fair and lovely in my view as an angel of God. The fourteen years I served your father appeared to me merely like a few weeks, on account of the love that I bore you. When we were joined in the endearing relationship of husband and wife, I felt as if a new sun had risen upon the world; yea, in the light of your countenance I experienced a new life there. True, I felt distressed at your subsequent discontent, because of your having no children. Nay, your fretfulness on this account was natural; for it expressed the deepest and strongest instinct of the female heart: and I now feel that I was to blame in being sometimes so angry with you as I was, whilst giving expression to so natural a feeling.

"Oh, how little can people down in the world tell what things are really for their good, and what things are really for their evil! My life upon earth gives a vivid illustration of this. I thought that a more unfortunate occurrence could not have happened to me, than to be forced to leave my mother and my father's house, and to be cast out a poor wanderer upon a desolate world. But, had this not taken place, I would never have met with you. We would never have been associated together in the relation in which we *once* stood to each other, and I would not at this moment feel that heaven is, if possible, dearer to me because I am privileged to share its joys in company with my beloved Rachel.

"*Your* life, Rachel, upon earth, also gives a very striking illustration how little God's people can tell what is for their good, and what is for their evil; and, consequently, it would be well if they were to look more than they do to the leadings of God's providence with them, and were to trust more to the wisdom of his holy appointments with them, than they feel generally inclined to do. Still you wept and fretted your life away because God, in his holy providence, denied you children. God at last granted your wish. What then? Why, the very thing you so ardently desired became the means of your death, parted you and me for a season, and left our dear little Benjamin without the care and love and unwearied attentions of a beloved mother. Oh! I recollect well the anguish I felt when forced to flee with you and with the rest of our family from your father's, and how much my distress was increased when you were overtaken in labor by the way. Sad and dark and dreary was our sorrowful separation. I felt as if the sun had left the sky, when I saw the light of your earthly existence go down, and as if the firmament had become a mourning pall to encircle the earth. But the night of our former sorrowful separation has now passed away. The glad and bright morning of a never-ending day has succeeded to it. Now we can look back upon our earthly troubles and trials, as our descendants, when settled in Palestine, looked back upon the bondage of Egypt, and upon the hardships and privations of the wilderness; yea, as the mariner, who casts anchor in the peaceful haven of his own dear native land, looks back upon the stormy ocean which he has left far in the distance behind him."

Rachel reciprocates: "Oh! I recollect well how painful our separation was to me when I was so unexpectedly parted from you, whilst we were on our way to the home of your youth. I remember well what a lonely feeling and desolate emotion spread over my soul, when I felt my heart and my flesh beginning to faint and to fail; when I looked, in my state of feeble exhaustion, upon the lovely face of our new-born babe, and wept at the thought that I was so soon to be taken from you and from him, and that our little darling was, alas! so soon to be deprived of all the kindly but nameless attentions of a mother's love. What a crush came down upon my heart, what a blight descended upon my earthly prospects, when I heard your voice beside me, and speaking to me in tones of love! But my fading and glazing eyes no longer beheld you. I heard our dear little babe breathing softly and sweetly upon the nurse's knee beside me. I asked him to be brought to me. I clasped him to my sinking bosom, and involuntarily looked down upon him to take my last parting view of him; but his little face was all enshrouded in darkness! I no longer saw it. Oh the reviving effect which it had upon my soul, whilst the dear ones in our home, and all the visible objects of earth, had become invisible to my benighted eyes; when I was struggling to get free from the body, and saw the bright and glorious morning of eternity beginning to break upon me; the great world of glory, that had previously been hidden from my view, coming, in all its splendor as it were, near to me, and when it flashed in all its loveliness full upon my gaze! Oh the delighted emotion that thrilled through my redeemed spirit, even whilst I was looking blindly upon you in your tears, and upon my little unconscious Benjamin, sleeping so peacefully, upon Joseph catching my almost lifeless hand, as if by that grasp he would keep me from going away! I took my seat in the chariot of salvation, whilst a company of rejoicing angels were around me to bear me up to my Father's home. Oh those ecstatic moments, when, hanging over that home in which I had left you in tears, and over the earth, which was already far beneath me, I looked down, and saw you standing at our tent-door, with your hand placed upon your brow, gazing down upon the ground in speechless agony and silent meditation over your loss! Yea, at the sight of you in that position, whilst the body I had left was lying behind you in the tent, a momentary feeling of sadness thrilled through my soul. It lasted only for a moment; for suddenly I heard the roll of the voices of the redeemed begin to fall upon my ear. My soul was full of rejoicings; for I knew that I was now near to my Father's home. But what was all this to the feelings that streamed through my spirit when I first entered the world of glory, was introduced into this heaven of love, stood within the veil that separates eternity from the sorrows of time, and beheld all those scenes that are so bright around us burst upon my view? But even that — what was it to the rapture of first beholding God? I had often listened to you speaking about the God of Israel; but how different the unveiled reality from all that poor mortals can conceive of it while the spirit is yet in the body!

"I became familiar with the scenes of heaven. I felt no impatience; for all here is holy resignation to our Father's will: but a feeling of ardor reigned in my soul, that you were come home to share these joys with me, to walk with me through these plains, to climb with me these hills, to perambulate with me these paths that converge towards the throne of God, and to join with me, and with all the throngs of heaven, in raising high the song of praise to Him who is the centre of all.

"And when it was announced here, that a company of angels, by God's appointment, had left these courts for earth to bring you home, and after the angels had left, how elevated beyond the aspirations of earth the thought that I was so soon to see you again! How ineffable the start of holy joy when the cry was raised, that Jacob was coming, and was already near! When you entered heaven, encircled and escorted by the multitude of angels; when you took your place for a little near to the throne, and was crowned by Jesus with that glorious diadem that now gleams upon your brow,—how the whole recollections of the past rushed upon my soul!

"How refreshing to my spirit the account you gave me of our family; of my once dearly-beloved sons, Joseph and Benjamin, as they affectionately wept over your dying bed, and tenderly kissed your brow, and pressed your feeble hand! Ah! heaven was sweet to me before you came; but it is, if possible, more joyful to me now; for we can not only enjoy, but reciprocate: and we have now the glad proof, that our remembrance here of our trials and sorrows upon earth, so far from lessening our happiness, is one of the chief elements that will enhance it through eternity."

CHAPTER VIII.

COMMUNION OF SAINTS IN HEAVEN (*continued*).

THE train of fancy in which I have been indulging — so consonant to our aspirations, so enchanting to our hopes, and yet not adverse to our reason, if not to a great extent favored by it — may be continued through other pictures. Take David, the sweet psalmist of Israel, and Jonathan, who loved him as his own soul, and cannot be parted from him in heaven. They discourse together of the clouds and darkness that hang in the view of men upon earth, and make inscrutable there the ways of God's providence.

"How dark and perplexing," may David now serenely say, "many of my heavenly Father's dispensations and actings appeared towards me in the world we have left! God lifted me up, I often thought, just that he might cast me down again. In the midst of the changing vicissitudes of my life, I was sometimes led to wonder if the great God, who walks in providence and deals out to his people their portion, was capricious and fickle. I now see these earthly dealings with me very differently in the light of eternity. It is the frowning sky and the appearance of the coming storm that lead the mariner to make all sail towards the haven, and urge the traveller to hasten to the covert. So now I see that it was because of the deceitfulness of my heart, that God, in his infinite wisdom as well as infinite love, spread around me the checkered scenes of my earthly experience.

"I was young, and comparatively thoughtless, when the Prophet Samuel came and anointed me to be the future king of Israel, in the room of your earthly father, who was then reigning. I felt my heart puffed up with pride at the thought of the dignity which thus awaited me. God saw this, and in love brought into operation means to humble me, — the jealousy and cruel hatred of your father; the bitter opposition of my enemies, who swarmed on every side wherever I turned; the many wearisome days and sleepless nights I spent homeless and cheerless, hunted like a partridge upon the mountain-top.

"Then, when God had placed me upon the throne, and opened the hand of his bountiful goodness so liberally, and showered down upon me so many blessings, both temporal and spiritual, my heart was again lifted up in the pride of a dangerous security; and thus, in an unthinking and thoughtless moment, I fell into the deepest of sins, and gave occasion to the enemies of the Lord to blaspheme. The sword of the Lord God was then unsheathed against my house; and ever after its gleaming edge hung over it, sharpened and made ready for the slaughter. How often I look back upon these dark transactions, with feelings of wonder that I could have lulled myself into such a state of hollow confidence and deceitful peace! I forgot that the holy eye of the all-seeing God had been turned towards me, and was glaring upon me during the whole of these iniquitous scenes in which I had been the chief actor.

"How can I describe that scene, when, sitting quiet in my palace, composed and calm, the Prophet Nathan was introduced to me?—how, after observing that in the sweet calm of that summer's afternoon the God of Israel seemed to be smiling upon his people, he began to recite to me, in well-set phrase and in beautiful elocution, the parable of the poor man and his ewe-lamb, and the conduct of his rich neighbor in robbing him of it?—how I was so unmindful of my own doings, and so stirred by the simple but graphic narrative of the prophet, that I hastily said, 'As the Lord liveth, the man that hath done this thing shall surely die'?—how Nathan then looked me broad in the face, pointed his finger towards me, and, with an emphasis and solemnity of voice that went to my very heart, said, 'Thou art the man'? These words sounded in my ears during the whole days of my pilgrimage on earth. The moment I heard them, the whole enormity of my conduct flashed upon my view; nor know I what I would have done, if I had not found refuge in prayer. Oh! what a privilege to those on earth that God has made himself known as the hearer of the stricken heart, and that they are permitted to unbosom their misery to his mercy! It was only when I poured out my heart before God with many tears, that the darkness of a deep and dreadful night passed from my soul, and that the morning of a joyful day began to dawn upon my heart. Yes, the dark clouds of sorrow were dispersed, and in the light of God's countenance I saw the evidence that I was forgiven.

"How little can those who are in the world foresee what effects are to follow particular actions, and how necessary it is to be always in a state of holy watchfulness! I little thought, when I rose from my bed to take a walk upon the roof of the king's house on the evening-tide in which I fell, that one short and hurried look was to change the whole current of my after-life.

"In the midst of all my distresses upon earth, I found a solace in solemn poetry. I wrote my psalms chiefly with the object of putting upon record my own varying spiritual experience, to show to the children of Israel in what the life of God in the soul really consists. I found that the soul in a state of grace was not as a calm, clear sky without a cloud, nor as a lake unstirred by the passing winds: it was as a sky sometimes clear, sometimes covered with clouds, sometimes filled with the warring winds and with the rolling thunder. Such was my spiritual experience in the world. I was sometimes in darkness, sometimes in light, and sometimes like the dim morning light spread over the mountains, whilst their tops were hung round with the drapery of clouds. I was at one time in doubt; and at another I felt in the glow of a comfortable assurance. I was at one time far down in the depths, as if cast off by God, and sunk into the floods; at another, elevated upon the hill-top of comfort and of heavenly hope, the whole firmament around me lighted up with the sunshine of God's favor and love, and the warm heavens above me opening to receive me into their eternal rest. I have given in the psalms my varying spiritual experience, for the instruction and comfort of the children of God in every age of the world. And what a solace has been to me my spiritual outpourings! These psalms, which, but for my sins, would never have been written, have been introduced into almost every congregation of God's people upon earth, as a part of their worship. Thus the spiritual Israel of God, singing them by the way, have been returning and coming to the heavenly Zion with songs and everlasting joy upon their heads; and now we find that the singing of God's praises in the world is the symbol and the preparation for celebrating the same holy aspirations in heaven."

Jonathan's recollections of God's providence: "I quite concur. The views you have expressed—that, in his dealings with his people in the world, God often enshrouds himself in a pavilion of thick darkness, that his judgments are a great deep, and his ways past finding out—are also mine. How mysterious did God's doings once appear to me also, when he deprived me of the kingdom of Israel, and gave it to you! But I now see that God in this acted towards me, not only in infinite wisdom, but also in infinite love. The natural pride of my heart was so great, that I believe, had I succeeded my father and ascended the throne of Israel, I must inevitably have lost my soul. God in love deprived me of an earthly kingdom in time, that he might confer upon me through eternity this heavenly one; yea, this crown of glory which I now wear, and which will never fade away."

Another picture of love is Mary Magdalene, and Mary the mother of Jesus. They, too, are recalling to their remembrances the scenes of the past, and are speaking to each other about the transactions of earth. "How glorious is heaven," may the first, who had been so inured to grief, now say, "compared with earth! and how joyous is our experience here, compared with what we passed through when in the world! Oh! when I look in love upon my blessed

Saviour upon the throne of sovereignty yonder, and now clothed with such transcendent honor and glory, I often recall the spectacle that I once witnessed upon earth, so distressing to my bleeding heart,—the scene of Calvary, — Jesus upon the cross, that crowned Saviour dying. Yea, I saw my dear Redeemer, whom I loved so ardently, nailed to the cross, and his precious blood crimsoning the ignominious tree! Oh the emotions of that dark hour, when I stood beside you in the midst of the congregated and insulting crowd, and beheld Immanuel suffering for those who were turning his sufferings into mockery! I saw that brow, which is now encircled with a diadem of glory, covered with sweat and blood, lacerated and torn with the cruel crown of thorns! — these eyes, that are now so mild, whose every look upon us here is love, and which had often looked upon me with the expression of a holy and heavenly favor, red with weeping, dim with sorrow, and closing in death! — these holy lips, which teach us here the high things of God, and drop like the honeycomb, pale with pain and the loss of blood, and quivering in the agonies of dissolution!—these feet, which traverse here the plains of bliss whilst feeding us with the manna of heaven, and leading us to the fountains of living waters, which I once washed with my tears, fastened with the bloody nails to the painful tree!—these hands, that now hold the sceptre of universal dominion, so often stretched forth upon earth to relieve the needy, or lifted up in prayer, stretched and nailed to the bloody beam! It was almost like a relief to me when the darkness began to mantle the sky, and to throw its deepening shadows over the earth; for it hid from my sight my dear Redeemer's contortions and twitchings of pain; just as it is sometimes like a relief to a mother to see her dear babe at rest in death, and its sufferings over. What horror streamed through my soul when I heard the voice of agony exclaiming, 'My God, my God, why hast thou forsaken me?'

"The resurrection-day will not be more joyful to me when it dawns, and when I will receive my body from the tomb, fashioned like to my dear Redeemer's, than was that morn when Jesus rose from the dead, and appeared to me in my sorrow in the garden. Oh the joy of my soul when I heard his well-known voice again saying to me, 'Mary!' I love to dwell upon the recollection of these scenes; for this awakens my gratitude to Jesus anew, and, by contrast, enhances my present happiness. Thus the remembrance of the sorrows and trials of earth is one element by which the joys of heaven are heightened to us here; just as the recollection of the temporal death all endure when we enter this great world leads us to appreciate aright the gift of eternal life which we now enjoy."

The mother of Jesus, in tones of love: "How often I too, amidst our present joys, recall the scenes of sorrow to which you have now referred! A mother's heart was bleeding as well as yours, when Jesus, now so gloriously exalted upon the throne, was upon the cross. What tender sensibilities awoke at the words, 'Behold thy mother!' My soul magnifies the Lord, my spirit rejoices in God my Saviour, because these trials are all past, and because all my earthly cares and solicitudes and anxieties are over now. I was highly honored by God whilst a daughter of earth, inasmuch as all the promises of a coming Saviour concentrated in me, and I was selected, among the thousands of women throughout Palestine, to give birth to Immanuel, who is God with us. But my name, I know, has been injured, and my dear Redeemer has been grievously dishonored, by a portion of the Christian Church paying to me, on this account, a misplaced reverence and an impious worship. Oh that they knew as well as I do that I did not save myself, and that I cannot save them, having no more power to bestow salvation upon the perishing than the meanest saint in glory, and would worship the Lord their God and serve him alone! Jesus himself has said, 'Whosoever shall do the will of my Father which is in heaven, the same is my brother and sister and mother.' Yet the poor heathen cries to his idol in his distress, and the poor idolatrous worshippers of a woman cry to me, and ignorantly worship me, who am not the hearer of prayer, and cannot answer it. Would that the nations of earth heard the voice and would listen to the proclamation of yonder angel who is now flying with outspread wings through the midst of heaven, and whose message is, 'Fear God, and give glory to *him*, and *worship Him* that made heaven and earth, and the sea, and the fountains of waters'! No, my privilege in this heaven of love is not to bestow salvation upon others, but to magnify and to praise my God and Saviour for the great salvation, which, through his shed blood, he has conferred upon me."

How interesting another picture, that of Paul and Onesimus! They are engaged in conversation. They are discoursing of God's sovereignty in grace, and of the overruling decrees, in reference to each of them, of God's electing love.

Paul's reminiscences: "In the possession of this heaven of love in which we have now our home for eternity, I often recall the past, and meditate upon the various manifestations of God's great and awful sovereignty in the salvation of men. What an illustration of the doctrine of grace does my salvation give! I was a proud and contemptuous Pharisee. Imagining myself righteous, I despised others. I was a blasphemer and a persecutor. I hated to hear the very name of Jesus. In my ignorance and ungodliness, I thought I was doing God service by persecuting all who called upon Him, the Father, in the blessed name of Immanuel. Surely, in these circumstances, I deserved to be left to perish. But God, who is rich in mercy, for his great love wherewith he loved me, did not leave me in my guilt. In the midst of deserved wrath, he remembered me with undeserved mercy. Jesus, in the sovereignty of his grace, appeared to me on my way to Damascus, and snatched me as a brand from the everlasting burnings. Oh! I feel as if eternity will be too short to utter forth the high praises of Him who thus looked down upon me in love, made bare his holy arm for my salvation, and compassed me about with a great deliverance. Yea, I was hanging, with the dark thunder-cloud of God's wrath above me, over the pit of eternal destruction, every moment about to perish for ever, when Jesus came down from this heaven of love, flew in his chariot of light and glory, encircled me in his covenant embrace, placed my feet upon the Rock of ages, and put a new song into my mouth, even salvation to my God. Thus elected to life, and to enjoy his favor, and to partake of the outgoings of his grace and love, I was not yet exempt from sufferings. My whole life upon earth was a scene of endless trials. I had no rest, few friends, many enemies, bitter and cruel. Wherever I went, the world was up in arms against me. I was like the petrel, flying always in the midst of the raging and warring winds, and among the rolling and dashing billows. A rough passage, indeed, to this eternity of rest, was mine; but when I reached this haven of eternal repose, and cast anchor within the veil, and looked back upon the foaming billows of time rolling in the distance behind me, I was recompensed, secure in the haven of eternity.

"I stood upon the shore of Melita after a fearful shipwreck, and saw the white waves breaking harmlessly at my feet. I then felt glad. I was gladder when I reached the shore of Immanuel's land, leaving behind me my poor shattered body lying stranded upon the shore of mortality. I often think that I could not have enjoyed heaven so much as I do, if I had not previously been subjected to a life of such sorrows, trials, and persecutions.

"Little did my bitter enemies think, when they were hunting me to death and stirring up the world against me, that they were pouring into the cup of affliction they placed in my hand a draught of comfort and of joy which I will drink for ever. It was this that led me to say whilst in the world, 'I reckon that the sufferings of this present time are not worthy to be compared with the glory which shall be revealed in us.' 'For our light affliction, which is but for a moment, worketh for us a far more exceeding and eternal weight of glory.' The view of the grated cell and the erected scaffold is the very thing that thrills the bosom of the criminal with rapture when his sovereign cancels the sentence, and pardons. Rising from the sick-bed upon which the poor patient has been stretched for a season, with the burning fever drinking up the moisture of his body, is the very thing that gives virtue to the cooling breeze which a summer's afternoon breathes upon the yet partially heated cheek. The sufferings of slavery give zest to the joys of liberty, and the experience of the perils and horrors of war weaves a wreath around the waving olive-branch of peace. So do I feel that my toils and sufferings in the world heighten the enjoyment of the blessings of heaven.

"I often think, Onesimus, upon the act of God's sovereignty and electing love in your salvation, as well as in my own. When I appealed to Cæsar, whilst standing at Festus' judgment-bar, I little thought that God was thus leading me, by a way that I knew not, to become the instrument of your salvation. But so it was. God was looking down in love from that throne upon which he is exalted. He saw you an unawakened and guilty sinner at Rome, and he had even then thoughts of mercy towards you. He brought me into perplexities and troubles that he might bring you salvation. I felt much annoyed at being detained so long in Rome before my appeal was decided by the emperor; but God was detaining me there till the set time for your deliverance should come. I remember well the moment when I first looked upon you among the auditors who were listening to me preaching in my own hired house. The tears were streaming from your eyes, as those eyes were fixed intently upon me. I had been preaching of righteousness and temperance, and was dwelling upon the awful fact, that there is a judgment to come, when suddenly you cried out, 'What must *I* do to be saved?' I cannot describe to you the thrill of joy that question sent to my soul. I saw that God was blessing his gospel, preached even in the midst of bonds and imprisonment. How joyful I felt when I met you alone, after the rest of my hearers had withdrawn, and when I discovered, that, encircled as you had previously been by a very ocean of ungodliness, you had found the pearl of great price, and become the new creature of God in Christ Jesus! I knew that the whole heavens were at that moment rejoicing over your spiritual birth; and it was with a heart filled with gratitude to God, that I knelt with you, and we lifted up our tribute of thanksgiving and of praise. Oh, with what a gush of holy fervor in my soul I then blessed him, that he had brought you into a knowledge of the truth as it is in Jesus; that he had sent the rod of his strength out of Zion, and that you had become willing in the day of your Redeemer's power!"

It is not difficult to figure the answer of Onesimus: "*Oh that sovereignty of God in the salvation of man!* Those in the world feel *God's decree* to be a *sea* which the *short line* of their *reason* cannot fathom; but God *is* sovereign in his electing love. I am an example of this. What had I done to deserve his favor and love? I had robbed my master, fled from his service, and run away from a home in which I had uniformly been kindly treated. I came in my wanderings to Rome, the metropolis of the world, and was glad when I reached that densely peopled city; for I thought it was scarcely possible for my injured master to find me there and bring me to punishment. I mingled for a season with the ungodly in that city of iniquity; and it was only casually I heard from a companion, that an eloquent prisoner had come up from Palestine upon an appeal to the emperor. I made inquiries, and learned your name. I had heard you preach whilst yet in the house of Philemon; but the word preached was not then carried home by the Spirit to my heart in its saving power. I thought I would like to see you again, that I might observe whether or not you were much altered in your appearance since the time when I saw you in Asia Minor. I thus came to hear you preach; but it was out of mere curiosity, and with no intention of making myself known to you. When I looked upon you in the midst of your persecution, — so calm and resigned in your bonds to the will of our heavenly Father, and exhibiting such an air of holy confidence and heavenly comfort upon your countenance, — I began to feel, even before you commenced your address, that assuredly you were engaged in the cause of truth. Oh! I will bless God through all eternity, that, by the invisible leadings of his providence, he brought me to hear you that day. Your words went home to my heart like winged arrows barbed with steel. The Lord Jesus was in the chariot of his preached gospel, and I felt the powers of the world to come. I awoke into a state of new existence, — into a life of light and liberty and holy joy."

CHAPTER IX.

COMMUNION OF SAINTS IN HEAVEN (*continued*).

TAKE another group, composed of Mary, Martha, and Lazarus, and listen to the first: "I often here recall the fond remembrances of our once-happy home at Bethany. Life upon earth is soon over, with its rainbow-hopes and its often anxious fears; but the *remembrances* of life will never be exiled from the chambers of memory. The scenes of Bethany are as fresh and as vivid before me *now* as they were when we lived there. I never hear the word 'Bethany' pronounced here, even in this home of love, but a whole flood of hallowed and tender associations connected with it are awakened in my soul. It was to us the house of God, the very gate of heaven. Our earthly parents left us whilst yet young. When they forsook us, the Lord took us up. I often recall with wonder and delight that afternoon, when Jesus, the Son of God, first came to our home, apparently a mere homeless stranger, and when I had first the privilege of hearing his voice. We felt in that divine and holy presence as if heaven had actually come down, not only into our home, but into our very hearts. Such serenity, such peace, such holy joy! How gladdened I was by the thought, that we were the objects of his love! and, in my too high spiritual security, I imagined no evil would come nigh our dwelling, and no cloud would ever in its darkness gather over it. O Lazarus! I recollect well what a blight came over my heart, when I looked upon you breathing with difficulty, and the perspiration in cold drops falling from your pallid brow. Approaching your bed softly, for you had become calmer, I thought you were asleep; and the sunshine of a momentarily awakened hope dawned upon my sorrowful heart. I thought the Lord was looking down upon us in love, and that you were to be spared to us. You tried to lift your head, and lay it upon your hand, whilst your elbow rested upon the pillow. You were unable to support yourself in that position, and you laid yourself down upon the pillow again. You then said, 'Is that you, Mary?' Your eyes had become so dim, that you did not see me; and you asked me to call for Martha, who was busily engaged in getting the drink you loved ready for you. What emotions of sorrow circulated through our souls, when you told us, as we were stooping over you in tears, that you felt yourself dying, and then, with a tremulous voice, commended us to the God of our salvation; adding, as you shook hands with us, 'We have been happy together in this home of love: but, oh! we will be happier when we meet up yonder, in our Father's home in heaven; for then we will have no sin, we will be perfectly holy, and I will not be a suffering patient to give you pain'! We sat down beside you, and looked on in silence, and beheld with you and towards you the doings of the Lord. You went to sleep; and oh the agony of that moment when we knew that from that sleep you would never awake,—that your spirit had passed away! Then were we desolate, for we felt that we had but few friends left; and this was the very cause that led us to look up in prayer, resignation, and hope to our Father in heaven, who lives whilst friends die.

"Nor was our grief yet ameliorated. Our sympathizing neighbors had stretched and dressed your body; and I approached the bed, laid my fevered hand upon your brow, and shook as I felt the coldness of death. I looked out from our desolate home, and thought the pale moon in the sky was sick with grief, and that the stars were silently weeping over the desolation of our hearts; but oh that morning of joy which broke upon our souls when we listened to the voice of Jesus at your tomb, saying, 'Lazarus, come forth,' and when you rose into life, and walked from the tomb to meet us, and came home with us and our friends, and again occupied your accustomed seat! We met that day in joy, but we met to be parted again; and how delightful is the thought, that we are now in a home that death will never enter, and where we will never be separated more!"

Martha's reciprocating views: "I now see that I felt, while in the world, far too anxious about what I was to eat, and what I was to drink, and wherewithal I was to be clothed; whilst indeed I gave myself no rest either by night or by day, planning my worldly arrangements, and bustling about to get them executed. I felt as if the world would necessarily stand still, and the sun would cease his journey through the sky, and the moon and stars would not remain upon their watch-towers, if I was not panting and sweating and hurrying to and fro in the performance of duty, and in carrying forward my domestic arrangements. 'Martha, Martha, thou art troubled about many things; but one thing is needful.' These words were to my bosom like the 'Peace, be still!' to the Sea of Galilee. They not only calmed my agitated heart, but caused the morning of a new day to break upon my soul. I then began to see that the world would go on when I was at rest in my grave; that the time would come when our household arrangements, which had almost entirely engrossed my attention, would be performed by the hands of another; and that there was something higher to live for than the world, and all that was in it. I saw that I had received life, not to spend it merely in the performance of worldly duties, but to dedicate it to God, and to make preparation for eternity.

"In the midst of these musings, a new light dawned upon my soul, — a new world came into my view. I felt then a peace and a calm descend upon my heart which I had never experienced before. I entered the pavilion of God's covenanted presence. I felt myself embowered in the embrace of my heavenly Father's love, and I too hastily inferred that care and anxiety would never be the inmates of my bosom again. I thought with Mary, that as Jesus loved us, and as we were the children of the living God, he would surely exempt us from affliction and trouble. Oh, what a shock these improper hopes received when we looked upon you sickening, and when we saw you, a brother beloved, numbered with the dead! How utterly empty and desolate and dark the world had become, as if the previously bright sun of our earthly comfort had set, and a dark and starless night of sorrow had gathered, with its clouds and stillness, around our desolated home! But when, in answer to our dear Redeemer's call, I heard the rustle of your dead-clothes; when I saw you rise up, and become erect again upon your feet; and when I looked upon you walking among the living with these grave-clothes still about you, — indeed, life from the dead, — I felt all that emotion of joy and of gratitude to the Son of

God, described by Mary, and which never can be forgotten even among the joys of heaven."

The loving response of Lazarus to these hallowed recollections: "We have left the earth, with its changing seasons and its varying spiritual experiences, for this heaven, in which one summer of life continually smiles, and in which our souls are always glad beneath the sunshine of God's unveiled countenance. I remember well the occasion to which you have both alluded. I felt pained, when the burning fever spread its withering fire over my body, at the thought that I was to be parted from you, with whom I had lived so happily; but this was changed into emotions of joy when I came up here to find a home of love. But how can I describe my feelings when commanded by God to leave heaven, and to enter my body again, and to return to you in your home of sorrow, in answer to the prayer of Jesus? When I saw again the sun; when I descended, and came within sight of the earth, as it rose before me, with its mountains and oceans and streams and woods and valleys; when I came within sight of Bethany, and saw Jesus standing at the mouth of the tomb in which my body was lying; when I saw you two standing beside him, and weeping; and when I beheld the multitude who were gathered around,—these things are for the spirit, rather than for the words of the spirit. Nor more adequate to the conception would be the description of my emotions when I entered my body again,—so like, in a mean sense, a person returning to his home after an absence, and finding the windows closed, the fires out, and silence and darkness reigning in every apartment,—and when I came out from the tomb, and returned with you to our home of love. I had to die the second time; but that death did not appear such a strange thing: and when I rose again, and came along the path that leads to this home, I felt like a person upon a road that is familiar to him, or like a child returning along the well-known path that leads him back to his father's home."

OBJECTIONS NOTICED.

Before closing this chapter, I will notice three objections that possibly *may* be brought by the captious against some of the views that I have advanced in setting forth *the communion of saints* in heaven.

Do you say, that, in the *pictures* I have given of the *family intercourse* in our Father's home, you have got a glimpse of a totally *different* heaven from that which you were previously, by faith, in the habit of looking up into? This *may* be, and nevertheless the heaven I have *described* may be the very heaven of the Bible. Again: if you say that I have represented the glorified who are in heaven as holding and enjoying *too great a familiarity* in their intercourse with each other, I would like you to give to the world the benefit of a distinct statement of the *proof* of your objection. *Is heaven a home? Do all who are in heaven constitute but one family?* Then surely it is fair *analogical, nay, it is logical, reasoning* to infer, that the intercourse which exists amongst the children of a pious Christian family upon earth is an *index* and a *symbol* of that which exists in heaven. Moreover, if you say that you had always previously pictured heaven in your imagination as a place whose inhabitants are so much engaged in the *realization* of the *beatific vision,' looking upon God, beholding the face of Jesus, and joining in the worship of Him* who sitteth upon the throne, that they have no *leisure and no opportunity of holding such fellowship with each other as I have depicted*,—do you really, then, believe that your eternity is to be spent in one continuous, fixed, and unchanging gaze upon God's face?—a position which would involve the conclusion, that all the inhabitants of heaven, and all its glorious scenery,—for I have shown it is a place,—are to be entirely hidden from your view as you thus stand transfixed and immovable. This is not the position of angels. They veil their faces with their wings before God, and go forth to execute his messages both of wrath and of love. This is not the position of those glorified ones from earth who are already in heaven. "They follow the Lamb whithersoever he goeth," and join in the high praises of eternity. The poor Brahmin takes his stand upon his lofty pedestal in the exercise of his superstitious worship; he withdraws his eyes from earth and from all terrestrial objects; he lifts them upwards, and fixes them, not upon God, not upon heaven, nor upon heavenly things,—for these are all unknown,—but upon the natural sun; and this he continues until he becomes entirely blind. This unchanging gaze upon what he calls God is the Brahmin's heaven. The Bible heaven is a home; and those who are in it constitute one united and happy family, whose *chief element of joy*, it is true, is *communion with Father, Son, and Holy Ghost*, but whose *secondary source of happiness*—a happiness not the less real—is the *fellowship* and *intercourse* which its members are permitted *to hold with each other*.

If heaven be a home, then it must be a place of sociality, of intercourse, and of fellowship. That would be a strange home in which the inmates had no social intercommunion. If your previous view of heaven be correct, and if the inmates of it be living in a state of separated, cold, and distant isolation from each other, the Holy Spirit, who speaks the truth in the Bible, would have given it another name,—perhaps a *penitentiary*, certainly not *our Father's house*. The communion which the members of God's family enjoy with each other in heaven, is, I grant, a source of joy subordinate to that which they hold with God; but just as communion with each other exists amongst the members of a family upon earth, so a holy communion also exists amongst the members of God's family in heaven.

I have, in my preceding observations, *assumed* the *fact*, that friends *do* recognize each other when they meet in heaven, which renders their fellowship there the more interesting and dear. I will afterwards give the *special proof* for this assumption.

CHAPTER X.

COMMUNION OF SAINTS IN HEAVEN, A SOURCE OF INSTRUCTION AND OF JOY.

HEAVEN is our home. Thus all who are there constitute but *one family;* for of Christ "the whole family in heaven and earth is named;" and, as the members of the same family, they have fellowship with each other. I believe that this fellowship which we will enjoy, when we enter heaven, with those who have reached it before us, will be to us a *source*, not merely of increased *enjoyment*, but of *instruction* also. The Bible is chiefly taken up in giving us a description of the evolutions of God's providence whilst watching over the human family during the long period of four thousand years, and of the various steps which he was led to take in order that he might effect our salvation. I believe that it will be a source both of instruction and of pleasure to meet those in heaven who were the leading agents under God in the accomplishment of many of those events which are described only shortly and darkly in the Bible; and to hear from their own lips, in the language of heaven, additional particulars respecting them.

How much more, for instance, could be declared of the mysteries of the creation than is contained in Genésis! How many conflicting theories indulged in by man might receive their settlement from the mouths of Adam and the patriarchs! And we are not surely to suppose that our curiosity as to these wonderful doings of God—amounting, as it does, to an aspiration—is to be left for ever as ungratified as it will be at our death. From Noah, who built the first ship and acted as the first sea-captain, how much might be learned on grand and mysterious events!—the circumstances connected with the coming of the deluge; what he felt when the waters were above the earth, and when he was sailing over the place where cities formerly stood; and what his feelings were when he came out of the ark, and looked forth upon a desolated world.

How much more, too, of these patriarchal times might be learned from Moses, besides what he has recounted of his own experiences!—what he felt in Egypt when the destroying angel was passing over it, and during that tedious wilderness-journey of forty years. And then there is that mysterious termination of his pilgrimage, when alone upon the mount on which he died, with no human being near him. We are curious to know more of the history of David, whose ways — detracting, in one instance, from the very embodiment of devotion — are to us, in many respects, inexplicable; a remark still more applicable to Solomon. We have all read the history of Samson, over and over again, as it is given in the Bible; but who has ever yet been able to form a definite and satisfactory view of his character, under its strange lights and shadows, with the gates of Gaza upon his shoulders? And then the pitiful picture he presents with both his eyes put out, groping for the pillars, upon which he pretended he was about merely to lean and rest himself. Perhaps his whole life was a riddle, and all that he did was just the acting-out of a strange parable, because his lot was cast among strange people.

I have often read the history of the Apostle Paul, the most enthusiastic and earnest and laborious of all the children of God, with his soul continually on fire, burning with an unquenchable zeal, and rapt in a conflagration of holy love and heavenly aspiration. If we feel so much interest in what we read of him, how much more would we experience in the full development of that abstruse spirit, a more complete insight into his character, and a more ample explanation of those wonderful doctrines, election and God's sovereignty in grace, which are yet to so many Christians a stumbling-block to faith, and to others a deep study of the mysteries of God!

Nor less interesting would be the personal experience of the Apostle John. What a gratification will it be to listen to his voice, giving an account of what took place that night, when the traitor rose from the table and left the holy brotherhood, and when Jesus, in the view of his approaching death, instituted the Lord's Supper, and spoke to the disciples about his Father's house of many mansions, where they were all at last to meet, and to spend an eternity of love together; but, above all, to hear him explain the Book of the Apocalypse, which has ever appeared to divines upon earth full of enigmas and riddles, a mysterious camera-obscura, a lofty but dark delineation of the future history of the Church of Christ!

We might thus go over all the patriarchs, prophets, and evangelists, every one of whom must have his soul replete with a knowledge which would be to us as a light in the dark, showing us the counsels of the Lord, and making plain to us his ways with his people; but what are we to say of all that region of ignorance which lies beyond the veil of mere phenomenal things, and to penetrate which has been man's effort since the creation of the world? We know that the triumphs of the greatest, in all the departments of science, are admitted by themselves to be no more than gropings in the dark. We know, too, that this ignorance is man's destiny; never to be changed while he is upon earth, and yet ever to be wrestled with under a hope that will never cease its aspirations. Nay, that very hope against despair is a sufficient indication to us that an explanation awaits us in another sphere, where the instruction will come from God, the angels, and the saints.

PART II.

Recognition of Friends in Heaven.

"THEN SHALL I KNOW EVEN AS ALSO I AM KNOWN."

CHAPTER I.

RECOGNITION OF FRIENDS IN HEAVEN.

THE recognition of friends in heaven follows *necessarily* from the two *facts*,—that heaven is a *home*, and that all who are in it constitute but *one* family. It would be a frigid home whose members were entire strangers to each other, and knew nothing of each other's present state and past lives.

Few subjects can possess an interest equal to that which is involved in this question: *Will friends, who have associated with each other upon earth, recognize each other when they rise from earth at death and meet in heaven?* It is of the deepest interest to all parents, to children, to partners, to brothers and sisters, to ministers, to their people, to masters, to servants, to companions, to neighbors. Without this recognition, heaven would not be a home of love. True, the present relationships in which we stand to each other upon earth will not be perpetuated in heaven. When an architect finishes his building, he takes down his scaffolding. These present relationships are a part of the flesh and blood, which, the Apostle Paul tells us, cannot inherit the kingdom of God. The Lord Jesus himself tells us, that the children of the resurrection — the glorified in heaven — neither marry, nor are given in marriage, but are as the angels of God. But, whilst we will not meet in heaven holding the *same relationship* to each other which we did upon earth, I believe we will know those there, when we rise and meet them before God unveiled, who are at present our beloved friends here.

It is somewhat strange, that this doctrine of the recognition of friends in heaven should ever have been called in question; but, strange as it may appear, there are some individuals who *doubt* it, and there are others who *deny* it. This, at least, cannot be denied, that in every pious heart there exists the *wish*, that the doctrine were true; for who, indeed, would like to part with those near and dear to them, at their death, never to see them more, so as to recognize them again?

It has been questioned, what would be gained by the non-recognition of our friends in heaven? It would be difficult to say; but I can tell what we would lose by it. We would lose the delight of meeting, in circumstances of peculiar gladness, those dearly-beloved ones from whom we were parted in our chamber of bereavement and sorrow; and we would be deprived of the joy of dwelling with those, through eternity, in a home which is a high realization of the last and dearest hope of dying humanity. Nay, there is something dreary and desolating and blighting to the warm, longing, social emotions of the heart, in the very supposition, that we *may* not, in a future state, recognize those we loved upon earth: and if the hope is to bear no fruit, then, in that case, I do well to bid them farewell at death; for, if there be not the recognition of friends in heaven, I am never to meet them so as to *recognize* them; and, in other words, I am parted from them for ever. They may exist; but they are *lost* to me, — *absolutely*, *eternally* lost.

Several *causes* are in operation, leading people either to *doubt* or positively to *discredit* this doctrine of the recognition of friends. Those who have married a second time are apt to think, that, were a first wife to meet and recognize the second, she would scarcely be able to look with heavenly love upon her successor: she would feel that she was not merely soon forgotten, but that her memory was injured by her husband's taking another to her bed; and to avoid this, to them, disagreeable meeting and recognition, such individuals take refuge in an entire disbelief of the doctrine. Their *wish* becomes the *proof*, that what they wish does not exist.

Some individuals, again, live with some of their friends such unholy lives upon earth, that they feel convinced that the remembrance of these lives, and the future recognition of their friends, will not contribute to their happiness above; and thus these also reason themselves into a disbelief of the doctrine. Others again, of a truly pious disposition, but whose devotion has too much of the transcendental about it, think that the saints in glory will be so occupied in the contemplation of God, in the worship of God, and in the enjoyment of the *beatific vision*, that the question, "Are our once dear friends here in the same home of love with us?" will have no interest to them. I have already shown this view to be both unscriptural and wrong.

Others imagine that the resurrection-body will be so changed and improved from what it was during life, that we will be no more able to recognize it than we could recognize a drop of water when changed into a flake of snow, or the little crawling grub when changed into the winged butterfly, as it sports with its rainbow-colors amid the beams of the summer's sun. Such individuals I believe to be wrong in their opinion respecting the *nature* of the change that the body is to undergo when it is raised from the grave on the resurrection-morning. The Lord Jesus is the pattern in all things of his people. When he rises from the tomb, he is not so changed that Mary Magdalene and the other women and his disciples do not know him,—

they recognize him at once; and so satisfactory does this peculiar example appear, that it does not seem necessary to say more.

Before setting forth in their order the *proofs* that have led me to believe firmly in the view that friends *will recognize each other in heaven*, I ask, May we not somewhat naturally infer, that, since the recognition of friends exists upon earth, which is God's, it is more than probable, apart from the proofs which demonstrate it, that recognition exists also in heaven, which is God's? Much of what exists upon earth should be looked upon by us as a symbol and visible representation of what is in heaven; and this is a natural inference, because the same God made both worlds, and reigns over them.

What is the Christian sabbath, with its holy rest and its hallowed and sublime associations? It is a *symbol* of the sabbath of eternity. What is God's public worship on his own holy day within the gates of Zion? It is a *symbol* of the high and everlasting public worship of God in heaven, in which all the hosts of glory exultingly join. What is prayer, in which exercise we look up to God, and make a direct address to Him who is our Father in heaven? It is a *symbol* of the beatific vision which saints in glory enjoy, and of the holy communion and inestimable privilege of speaking to God face to face, which those in heaven possess. What is the Lord's Supper and Christ's banqueting-house upon earth, in which the great Master of assemblies meets us, and breathes upon our souls the Holy Ghost, and puts into our hands the cup of salvation, and feeds our souls with the bread of life? It is a *visible representation* of what the glorified in heaven are enjoying, who are seated in Christ's banqueting-house above, in his own manifested and blessed presence, and at the table that will never be drawn. What is a Christian family, with its sympathy and love, and sweet and open intercourse existing among its beloved members? It is the *panorama* of God's great and happy family in heaven. Upon the same principle, I argue that the recognition of friends, after a short parting from them in this world, is just a *type* or a *symbol* of that which is taking place among friends when they rise at their death from earth, and meet in heaven beneath God's covenant-presence, and under the sunshine of God's approving love.

I now proceed to notice some of the sources of evidence for this recognition of friends.

PROOF FIRST. — RECOGNITION A DOCTRINE OF NATURAL RELIGION.

The recognition of friends in heaven is a dictate of natural religion. Even those who did not enjoy the light of revelation believed in it. The resurrection of the body is not a doctrine of natural religion. Apart from the revelations and the intimations of Scripture, the thought that the buried bodies of the dead are to be raised seems never to have entered the human mind. Panl is stigmatized as a babbler becauee he preached at Athens the resurrection of the dead. The view which unenlightened reason takes of the destiny of the *body* of man is, that, when it is committed by surviving and sorrowful friends to the cold bed of the grave, it is to sleep there for ever. The thought of a coming resurrection-morning, when the buried bodies of all the dead are to awake and to rise as Lazarus did at the call of Jesus, never gleamed in with its ray of comfort, apart from revelation, upon the dark and sorrowful heart of the bereaved. The heathen philosophers saw the nights suceessively pass over them; they saw the morning dawn: but the thought that a morning was coming to the grave never once entered their mind. The spring came, and breathed upon the earth with its generative warmth; the flowers sprang np around the human family: but the expectation of a spring coming to the grave never once suggested itself to the thoughts of the unenlightened reason of man.

It is different in reference to the soul. Apart from revelation, men have in all ages believed in the cxistence of the soul *after* death. Man's *immortality* is a doctrine of natural religion. Men in every age and in every clime have believed that the soul survives the shock of death, and lives after the body in which it once dwelt goes to sleep. Further, men have almost as universally believed in the doctrine of the *recognition of friends* in their disembodied state. *Immortality* and *this recognition* are the almost universal response of humanity. Examples will suggest themselves to the reader of history. The source of this universal belief *may* be either *tradition* or *desire for it*.

PROOF SECOND. — SCRIPTURE TEACHES RECOGNITION.

The Scriptures both assume and teach the doctrine of recognition. I may here allude to the *amount* of proof which we may reasonably suppose the Scriptures will afford in support of this tenet. There is a *principle* upon which God seems generally to proceed when giving us evidence in confirmation of any doctrine of his blessed gospel. Those doctrines that we feel *indisposed* to receive and believe, or which are calculated to *crush* the *pride* of man, are largely proved, and much insisted upon: such as those of human depravity; the incarnation of the Lord Jesus; the personality of the Holy Spirit, and his work of grace upon the soul of man; salvation by faith through the imputed righteousness of Christ alone; the resurrection of the body; the fulness and distinctness of the last judgment; the final and eternal separation of the righteous and the wicked; the exile of the lost into hell for ever; and the rising of the saved to enter heaven, to dwell there in a home of love for eternity.

Those doctrines of revelation, on the contrary, which we have a *predisposition* to receive and believe, are not so fully and distinctly set forth; such as the existence of God (a doctrine, in fact, which the Scriptures do not *prove*, but *assume*), the immortality of the soul, the beatific vision, the full and unveiled view of God above in his glory, the communion of saints and of angels in heaven through eternity as the members of the same family, our body after our resurrection bearing the exact and holy image of Jesus, the recognition of our friends in heaven.

There are many passages, both in the Old and also in the New Testament Scriptures, in which the doctrine is *assumed* and *incidentally* alluded to; such as, "Then Abraham gave up the ghost, and died in a good old age, an old man and full of years, and was *gathered to his people.*" "And Isaac gave up the ghost, and died, and was *gathered unto his people,* being an old man and full of days." "And, when Jacob had made an end of commanding his sons, he gathered up his feet into the bed, and yielded up the ghost, and was *gathered unto his people.*" To Moses, God says, "Get thee up, and die in the mount whither thou goest up, and be *gathered unto thy people;* as Aaron thy brother died in Mount Hor, and was *gathered unto his people.*" The expression, "gathered unto his people," does not refer to the bodies lying in the family tombs of those alluded to, but to the souls of their ancestors. The two mounts upon which Aaron and Moses respectively died and were buried were *not* the sepulchres of their ancestors.

The cave where Abraham was buried was *not* the sepulchre of his ancestors. David says, " I shall go to him; but he shall not return to me." " Hell from beneath is moved for thee, to meet thee at thy coming: it stirreth up the dead for thee, even the chief ones of the earth; it hath raised up from their thrones all the kings of the nations. All they shall speak, and say unto thee, Art thou also become weak as we? art thou become like unto us?" " Make to yourselves friends of the mammon of unrighteousness; that, when ye fail, they may receive you into everlasting habitations." Without quoting any more passages from the Bible in which the doctrine of recognition is merely *assumed*, I will now allude to a few in which it is directly and distinctly *taught*.

It is, perhaps, proper to make the remark, that even one direct statement made by God in the Bible is quite sufficient to prove the doctrine of recognition to the satisfaction of every one who reverences the word of inspiration. " Abraham said, Son, remember that thou in thy lifetime receivedst thy good things, and Lazarus evil things; but now he is comforted, and thou art tormented." This passage plainly teaches us that Abraham *recognizes* Lazarus, and *associates* with him, in the world of glory, *speaks* of him by *name*, and is familiarly acquainted with his *earthly history*. Christ's transfiguration scene teaches the doctrine of the recognition of friends. Moses and Elias, two glorified saints from heaven, appear there in *companionship*. The same subject engrosses the thoughts of both. They speak to Jesus of the decease which he was to accomplish at Jerusalem. The Apostle Paul thus addresses his Thessalonian converts: "For what is our hope, or joy, or crown of rejoicing? Are not even ye in the presence of our Lord Jesus Christ at his coming?" These converts could only *become* the apostle's joy by his *recognition* of them in Christ's presence. Jesus thus addresses his disciples who were sorrowing at the thought of his departure: "And ye now, therefore, have sorrow: but I will see you again, and your heart shall rejoice; and your joy no man taketh from you." The Lord Jesus here gives the intimation, that the disciples were to see him, and associate with him in glory; and, consequently, they were to associate with each other. The apostles knew Jesus when they met him after his resurrection. "The men of Nineveh," "the queen of the south," will be known and recognized at the judgment-throne, when they appear there as witnesses against the Jews who despised and rejected Jesus. It is not necessary to bring more Scripture proofs for this doctrine. This source of evidence is open to all who have the Bible in their hands. I will rather now proceed to give some evidences for the doctrine which are not so patent.

CHAPTER II.

RECOGNITION OF FRIENDS IN HEAVEN (*continued*).

PROOF THIRD. — HEAVEN A HOME PROVES RECOGNITION.

THE *fact that heaven is a home, proves, as I have already said, recognition.*

Those who live in the same home upon earth are not strangers; they have a knowledge of each other; an acquaintanceship and fellowship exist among them. It is the same in heaven. Those who are there are the members of the same family, and, as such, have free communication and intercourse. They are in possession of language; they can speak to each other; they can sing; they can both put and answer questions. "And one of the elders answered, saying unto me, What are these which are arrayed in white robes? and whence came they? And I said unto him, Sir, thou knowest. And he said to me, These are they which came out of great tribulation, and have washed their robes, and made them white in the blood of the Lamb. Therefore are they before the throne of God, and serve him day and night in his temple." "Then I heard one saint speaking; and another saint said unto that certain saint which spake, How long shall be the vision concerning the daily sacrifice, and the transgression of desolation, to give both the sanctuary and the host to be trodden under foot?"

Those who are in heaven are in possession of their *memories*. The souls under the altar remember the earth, and the death they endured upon it, as well as the *means* by which they were redeemed, — the blood of Christ. Those in heaven, as is manifest from many passages of Scripture, have a full remembrance of the past. With this faculty, I ask, granting that we will not have an *intuitive recognition*, How long will we live with them after our meeting there till we come to know those who had once *fellowship* with us in the bonds of a hallowed friendship upon earth?

Suppose you take up your lodging for a night in a hotel, and meet two strangers in the public room, with whom you take supper: if they be truthful and communicative, and if you enter into conversation with them, you will find that one single hour will not pass over you until you are put in possession of a pretty extensive knowledge of their past lives; to what country they belong, where they were born, what are or were the names of their parents; what brothers or sisters they have, with their names; if married, to whom; and what are the names of their children, through what countries they have travelled, what they have seen, and from what place they had come previous to the time when you met them.

The same facility for becoming acquainted with the past lives of those we meet exists in heaven. Knowledge is perfected there. How much more enlarged, then, will your acquaintanceship be with each other, when you, who are the children of God, come to meet, not for an hour at supper, but for eternity, in an abiding and unchanging home, and that in the presence of your common Father, and enjoying the freest intercourse with your blessed Redeemer, as well as with each other! By that free intercourse alone, even if no other mode existed, you will come to know those who were your bosom companions upon earth, who lived with you in the same home, who stood towards you once in the nearest and dearest relationships of life, who walked with you in the covenant of your God, with whom you took sweet counsel, and went up to the house of God in company.

PROOF FOURTH. — ANALOGY PROVES RECOGNITION.

Analogy proves that there will be the recognition of friends in heaven. Suppose the case of two brothers, who spent the morning of life together in their beloved parents' home. They wade the stream, and pull the flowers, and climb the trees, and search for nests together; they read God's Word at the family altar, and sing the same psalm in the same church. In God's providential dealings with them, these boys are separated whilst rising into manhood: the one embarks for Calcutta, the other for San Francisco. They do not meet, nor hear from each other by letter, for the long period of forty years. Suppose these two brothers were to leave respectively the land of their adoption, and were, unknown to each other, by one of those coincidences in the providence of God which we call chance, to meet in the same hotel at the Cape of Good Hope; suppose that they were so much changed in their appearance that they did not recognize each other, and were to enter into conversation: how short a time would pass over their heads until some expression would be used, some reference to the past made, or a question put respecting *where* they were born, *who* were their parents, *where* they had come from, and *whither* they were going, which would reveal to them the joyful and thrilling discovery that they were *brothers*, and that the same fond parents had watched over them in the days of their boyhood! How poor a case is this in comparison with a meeting in heaven, and yet with the points of analogy so well fitted, that we cannot escape the conviction, that the one is a type of the other!

How slight the touch from which recognition springs! Two young men entered the British army, who were fellow-parishioners in their boyhood; they enlisted in different regiments; they did not meet for many years. The two regiments were successively sent out to India, and they came incidentally to be stationed in the same town. These two young men were thus brought into each other's company occasionally, both upon parade and also in pleasure-excursions; but they did not recognize each other. One day, whilst together at the canteen, a fall of snow had taken place, which was succeeded by a cold, bleak, and drizzling rain. One of them happened casually to make the remark, "This is a Glentore thaw." The other, whose attention was at once arrested by the name of the locality referred to, asked him, "What do you know about Glentore?" This question led to an explanation, and that explanation resulted in the discovery, that they were not merely fellow-Scotchmen, but had been born in the same parish, had attended the same school, had stood in the same class, had played on the same village-green, and had worshipped God in the same church.

Grant that the glorified have the *gift of language* in heaven, and are capable of speaking to each other about the past; and this *must be conceded*, or some portions of the Scriptures must be rejected: how long will those who were friends upon earth associate and converse in their home of love and of fellowship in eternity, until some casual remark, or some reference to the past, or some question put, reveals to them the important discovery, that they once lived in the same home upon earth, were once the members of the same happy family, and spent life together in an earnest, persevering, and successful preparation for heaven?

Further, angels know each other; and they appear, from the narratives set before us in the Bible, to have a large and a very distinct knowledge of the members of the human family,—not those in heaven merely, but those also who are dwelling far beneath them, and distant from them, upon our planet. Why should the glorified not have a similar acquaintanceship with all the children of God in glory, as well as with those who still live down in the world? Have they not become perfected in knowledge, and like unto the angels? The angel who passed over the land of Egypt had no difficulty, so far as we are told, in selecting the first-born child in every home which he entered. I believe that messenger of woe did not commit during that painful night one single blunder, by killing a younger in mistake for the first-born child in the family. Nor can I read the inspired account of that memorable night, without feeling impressed with the conviction, that the whole population of Egypt was individually and minutely known to that angelic messenger, whilst hovering with the wings of death over that devoted land. The angel who released the Apostle Peter from prison had no difficulty in distinguishing *him* from all the rest of the prisoners who were confined in its different wards. The angel who breasted the fury of the Adriatic Sea, and, in his placid and peaceful descent from heaven, lighted upon the deck of that vessel in which Paul was sailing, and around which the waves were rolling mountains high, had no difficulty in singling out *him* from the rest of the passengers, and in making this announcement: "Fear not, Paul: thou must be brought before Cæsar; and, lo, God hath given thee all them that sail with thee." The angel who appears to Cornelius has a distinct knowledge of the Apostle Peter's movements, and of the house in which he was *lodged*, as is evident from this command: "And now send men to Joppa, and call for one Simon, whose surname is Peter. He lodgeth with one Simon, a tanner, whose house is by the seaside: he shall tell thee what thou oughtest to do."

If angels know the members of the human family so minutely, as the *facts* I have referred to clearly demonstrate, why should the members of the human family not know each other, and recognize each other, when they meet in a higher and more perfected state of knowledge, and become like to those angels in love and wisdom?

Abraham shows, in his address to the rich man in hell, that he has a *distinct* and *minute* knowledge both of *his* previous life, and of the life of *Lazarus*. We are not told *how* Abraham gained this knowledge; but surely the same source of communication and of information to which *he* had access is open to *all* the children of God. Moreover, the Lord Jesus Christ, during his sojourn here, was an exemplification in all things of the life which the glorified of God are living in heaven,—his humiliation and pains and sorrows excepted. Did the Lord Jesus, whilst here in the world, live in a state of isolation and estrangement from those who were round about him? Did he discountenance holy friendship, and frown upon it? Did he show in his earthly life, that the social affections did not exist in his bosom? The very reverse is the case. The Lord Jesus came down from heaven into this world to destroy *sin*, not to *annihilate friendship*, not to *eradicate* the *social affections* from the bosoms of his people. The disciples were the companions and the friends of their Lord and Master. He who is God over all, blessed for ever, condescended to speak to them, and to hold intercourse with them in all the familiarity of the most loving, holy, and intimate friendship. The members of the family at Bethany were the peculiar objects of the Redeemer's regard: "Now, Jesus loved Martha and her sister, and Lazarus." The Apostle John was known by the appellation, "the disciple whom Jesus loved." Mary Magdalene met Jesus after his resurrection, near to the tomb in which he had been laid, and became conscious it was he by the tone of endearment with which he pronounced her name. If the Lord Jesus thus cherished holy friendship whilst upon earth, and exemplified a peculiar attachment to particular individuals, and cultivated the social affections as they are exhibited in *our* friendships with *our* bosom friends, upon what principle, for what reason, will Christ's followers in heaven be stripped of that privilege?

And, lastly, if you deprive Christ's followers in heaven of their social affections, you strip them in a great measure of their religion: for love is a social feeling; and take away love from the bosoms of the saved, and what kind of a heaven will you leave?

CHAPTER III.

RECOGNITION OF FRIENDS IN HEAVEN (*continued*).

PROOF FIFTH. — THE WAY GOD'S CHILDREN ENTER HEAVEN PROVES RECOGNITION.

*ELIEVERS, at their death, enter heaven publicly and triumphantly; and this must be the source of recognition.*

I believe that a great misconception exists in the minds and views of many Christians respecting the way in which the children of God enter into heaven. The generality of Christians, if they think about the matter at all, have, some way or another, come to cherish the vague, visionary, and undefined view, that God's children ascend into heaven at death as silent, unperceived, and unnoticed as a current of air flows into a room, or as a new thought glides into our minds whilst we are sitting in the midst of a large company, without, of course, any one around us being at all aware of the entrance of the new-come stranger.

It is not *thus* believers at their death enter into glory.

I believe that the *way* in which the Lord Jesus entered heaven at his triumphant ascension, to take possession for eternity of the glory which he had with the Father before the world was, is just a *representation* of what takes place when a child of God enjoys that privilege. What were the circumstances in which the Lord Jesus left this world at his ascension, and rose, and entered into his kingdom? He left it as a conqueror leaves the battle-field, where he has overthrown his formidable foes, and returns home in the midst of the plaudits and shoutings of assembled multitudes. And did those who were in heaven not *expect* Christ's ascension, and make *preparation* for it? These passages of Scripture show that they did, and prove to us that Jesus entered heaven openly, triumphantly, and gloriously, observed and welcomed by all who were there, attended by many of its exulting inmates, who had come out to receive him, and, with the welcome of a joyous greeting, to hail him home. "God is gone up with a shout, the Lord with the sound of a trumpet." "Lift up your heads, O ye gates; and be ye lift up, ye everlasting doors; and the King of glory shall come in. Who is this King of glory? The Lord strong and mighty, the Lord mighty in battle. Lift up your heads, O ye gates; even lift them up, ye everlasting doors; and the King of glory shall come in. Who is this King of glory? The Lord of hosts, he is the King of glory." "I saw in the night visions; and, behold, one like the Son of man came with the *clouds* of heaven, and came to the Ancient of days; and *they* brought him near before him." "And when he had spoken these things, while they beheld, he was taken up, and a cloud received him out of their sight. And, while they looked steadfastly toward heaven as he went up, behold, two men stood by them in white apparel; which also said, Ye men of Galilee, why stand ye gazing up into heaven? This same Jesus, which is taken up from you into heaven, shall so come in like manner as ye have seen him go into heaven."

Look, again, at what takes place when Stephen dies. This is the description which the Holy Spirit gives us of his death: "But he, being full of the Holy Ghost, looked up steadfastly into heaven, and saw the glory of God, and Jesus standing on the right hand of God; and said, Behold, I see the heavens opened, and the Son of man standing on the right hand of God." Stephen's soul does not, when his body becomes inanimate, rise, and slip into heaven unnoticed and unobserved by those who are there; for Jesus, who is upon the throne, rises to welcome his faithful confessor up into the joys of his Lord, and stretches forth his arms to receive the beloved spirit. Nor can it be asserted, that no one in heaven, with the exception of Jesus, noticed Stephen at his entrance there. I believe, on the contrary, that there was not *one*, whether angel or glorified saint, who did not share in the interest which

Christ himself manifested, and who did not join in the open acknowledgment which Christ himself vouchsafed to him who was the first martyr of the cross.

What, then, happens when a believer falls asleep in Jesus? We may again have recourse to an earthly analogy. When a child is born, comes into the world, and is ushered into the domestic circle of a family where love and union and godliness reign, does no one in the house know of such an event? Do the doctor and the nurse, who act the part of attending assistants, know nothing about the matter? Are they asleep? Does the little stranger arrive, and increase the number of the home-circle, without observation, until, by something like mere accident, some one in the house happens to look to the little bassinet, and sees the stranger nestling there, dressed in white, lying asleep, and as tranquil as if Peace had come down from heaven to take its seat upon the throne of silence? The mother knows something about the arrival of the little one; and I suspect, moreover, there is not one individual in the home who does not anticipate the event, and share in the general excitement. Verily, the same thing takes place in our Father's home above, when a child of God is born to the inheritance of glory, rises at the hour of death from earth, enters into heaven, and becomes a member — not for time, but for eternity — of God's great and glorious family.

Again: death to the believer is his coronation. From this state of many trials and troubles, he goes to receive a kingdom, to ascend a throne, and to wear a crown, — a crown that shall never fade away. "Be thou faithful unto death, and I will give thee a crown of life." "To him that overcometh will I grant to sit with me in my throne, even as I also overcame, and am set down with my Father in his throne." It surely would seem strange for a sovereign to be crowned without any of his people either seeing or hearing of a ceremony, which, from time immemorial, has been attended with such demonstrations of worldly grandeur and exultation. And how much more illustrious is that high day in heaven, when a child of God rises from earth, more than a conqueror through Him who loved him, and enters into his kingdom, that he may be diademed with the crown of glory that is never to fade!

Some of these scenes of relationship, as they rise to the mind, transcend all our earthly experiences of pleasure. A father may ascertain that his own child is the individual crowned, and may hear her name upon the lips of all; hear her name announced as one worthy of that crown which she is to wear, and of the high place she is to occupy for ever. But does not our mind, so pleased with such ecstatic visions, reject the supposition, that that father shall not know that it is his daughter who is the object of all that demonstration?

Thus the public entrance of the children of God into heaven, the public announcement of their name as they enter to join the family of the blessed above, and the tide of new joy that rolls over the assemblies as a holy welcome given to the new-comer, *will secure* their recognition by their *friends who are there before them.*

CHAPTER IV.

RECOGNITION OF FRIENDS IN HEAVEN (*continued*).

PROOF SIXTH.—THE CONDITION OR STATE IN WHICH GOD'S CHILDREN ENTER HEAVEN AT DEATH MUST SECURE THEIR RECOGNITION BY FORMER FRIENDS WHO ARE THERE.

WHAT is that state? I will first mention what it is not. God's children do not enter heaven at their death inanimate, and deprived of the power of thought. They do not enter heaven leaving their *memories* and their *intellectual faculties* behind them. They do not enter heaven stripped of their *social affections*, and thus rendered unfitted for the companionship of God's children who are already there. They do not enter heaven *selfish* and *careless* about their once dear friends, who fell asleep in Jesus before them.

What, then, is the *state* in which the children of God enter heaven? They do so *living*, and with all the faculties of their souls retained and in full operation. It is the body merely that may be said to *die* at death: the soul *lives*, and even acquires new powers and susceptibilities whilst death is taking place. To the glorified, death is jubilee, — emancipation from sin and suffering and sorrow. God's children enter heaven, even as we may suppose an affectionate child that has been some time absent enters his or her father's home, to join the beloved circle who are dwelling there. They enter with the same *interest* about their past journey in life, and about the events that happened to them by the way, that the pilgrim feels when he returns to his dwelling, and gives an account to its members of all that he has passed through. They enter with the same eager curiosity after those who were dear to them upon earth, that the emigrant feels when he lands upon the shore of that country to which his father and mother and wife and children and brothers and sisters, and many other acquaintances and neighbors, sailed before him, and in which they are settled. Above all, God's children enter heaven at death with their *memory* in full exercise, and with a *full remembrance* of their past lives, and consequently of their former friends.

This is evident from various passages of Scripture. The rich man mentioned in the Gospels remembers his five brethren, *his* and *their* former life; and in the exercise of *judgment*, conjoined with *memory*, he infers that his five brethren are in danger of coming into the same place of torment. The whole of the passage connected with the rich man and Lazarus proves that those who are in the great world of eternity — both those who are in heaven and those who are in hell — have a full and distinct remembrance of the past.

To the lost, this remembrance is a source of misery: for they remember their day of grace squandered; their precious privileges misimproved; the offer of salvation put away from them; God trifled with, whilst he called them to repentance, and waited to be gracious, and wished to save them; Christ and his great salvation rejected and lost for ever.

To the saved, this remembrance of the past is a source of joy. Lazarus can thus compare his riches in heaven with his poverty upon earth, his exaltation in heaven with his degradation and outcast condition in life, his misery and wretchedness at the rich man's gate with the delights and joys of his Father's home.

It is difficult to say *why* the rich man made the request, that Lazarus should leave heaven for a short season, and visit his father's house upon a special mission of warning to his brothers. It might be made in sympathy. He might retain so much of the feelings of humanity, even in hell, as to lead him to pity the case of his five brothers who had been, during his life, encouraged in their path of guilt by his evil example; and he might honestly wish that they might be delivered from the awful doom to which he had been subjected. The request might also be made through a selfish motive. These brothers were perhaps seduced and led into sin through his example; and thus he might dread the sight and the presence of them with him in hell, lest this should add fuel to the fire with which he was consumed. The request of the rich man plainly implies that the lost remember the past. *They* have not lost their memories. Have the saved in heaven lost theirs? Abraham remembers the past, and reminds the rich man of his former good things which he had lost for ever. He remembers also the poverty of Lazarus upon earth, which had been exchanged for the riches of glory.

The passage in the Book of Revelation which I have already quoted, and in which the souls of the martyrs who are under the altar put this question, "How long, O Lord, holy and true, dost thou not judge and avenge our blood on them that dwell on the earth?" plainly proves that the glorified in heaven have not forgotten the scenes of earth. These martyrs, who appeal to the truth and to the holiness of God, remember the earth where they suffered, and the bloody death which they endured upon it at the hand of their murderers. If those, who have been cruelly put to death for the word of God and for the testimony of Jesus Christ, remember so vividly in heaven the bloody scene of their death upon earth, do the rest of the glorified not remember their peaceful death-bed? — the friends who surrounded them there, and who tried, with all the attentions which experience and love could suggest, to mitigate the sufferings of their last hours; the minister who spoke to them of *heaven as their Father's house, and of Jesus as the way to it*, and who prayed that God would manifest his covenant love to them, and sustain them by the riches of his grace when their heart and flesh began to faint and to fail, and that Jesus would vouchsafe his guidance to them to conduct them in safety to their eternal home of love; the last look they got of some beloved one, whom they saw bathed in tears, when their eyes closed upon all that is sublunary; when the dark night of death, suddenly coming down upon them, hid the whole material things that were around them from their view.

Yes, the whole countless multitudes of the saved who are with Christ in glory *remember* the homes where they once lived; where they were born from above, and became through grace the new creation of God in Christ Jesus; where they obtained peace with God, and liberty of access, through faith, into the grace wherein God's children stand. They *remember* all the way by which the God of their salvation led them whilst struggling here with giant evils. They *remember* the dear friends through whose conversation and advices and example and prayers they felt themselves advanced in the divine life, and prepared for that home of love which they have entered for eternity.

Every song which the redeemed in glory sing, commemorating in the praises of eternity the finished work of Jesus and the efficacy of his shed blood, shows that they have a *remembrance* of the past, that they are in full possession of the *faculty of memory.* Hence those ascriptions of praise to Jesus which they raise before the throne: "Thou wast slain, and hast redeemed us to God by thy blood, out of every kindred and tongue and people and nation." "Salvation to our God which sitteth upon the throne, and unto the Lamb." Can the glorified forget what they read in their Bibles about the shedding of Christ's blood upon earth, as they stand with Jesus in white upon the hill of the heavenly Zion? Do those who stood with the Apostle John upon the hill of Calvary, and who saw the blood of Immanuel crimsoning the cross, now forgot what they beheld there? Do all in heaven forget the time when the blood of Jesus was sprinkled by the Holy Spirit — if I may so express myself — upon the mercy-seat of their souls; when they obtained redemption through that oblation, the forgiveness of sin according to the riches of God's grace? Do they forget also the *means* which the God of their salvation *used* through the agency of the Holy Spirit to apply to their consciences and hearts the blood of atonement; the mother who first taught them to pray, and to ask for the new heart from God; the father who so often led their devotions at the family altar, and prayed for them to God that he would bestow upon them the great salvation that was in Christ Jesus, with all the unction and fervency of a holy earnestness; the minister who first, by his evangelical preaching, so full of love, nay, so full of Christ, led them to give heed to the things that belong to their eternal peace; the friend that was led by the constraining influences of a Saviour's love to speak to them *for* Christ and *about* Christ upon a particular sabbath evening, it may be, and in a particular room, when they for the first time tasted the word of God, and felt upon their souls the powers of the world to come?

It is said that this somewhat strange effect happens to a person in the act of drowning; for, some time preceding death, the events and actions of the individual's whole past life flash in full array upon the memory, as if a life-panorama were suddenly held up to view by an invisible hand. May this not be a foreshadowing of what takes place to every individual for some moments *before* dissolution, and through eternity *after?* Is it not *possible* that the soul of one a-dying leaves the fallen and motionless body, the weeping, bereaved relatives, the chamber of dissolution, and rises and enters heaven, with a far stronger *memory*, a *clearer*, *minuter*, and far more *vivid recollection* of the whole past of his life, than he ever possessed before? In heaven, we are to be made *perfect* in *knowledge*. *Memory* is the storehouse in which our knowledge is chiefly deposited. If, then, we are *deprived* of our memory, we would be led to wonder why it is that Christ has conferred upon us a reward, and why there are differences in glory among the saints in heaven.

Again: the children of God enter heaven in possession of their judgment, and with all their reasoning powers in full exercise. Surely no one supposes that God's glorified children are like those hibernating creatures, who, during winter, live in a dormant state, and that the resurrection-morning must first usher in the spring that is to be followed by an eternal summer before they awake fully to life and intelligence. Those who are in heaven have entered it in the full possession of all their *intellectual powers*, and they are *exercising* them.

They are doubtless comparing eternity that is now encircling them with the time that was, and will be no more; heaven that is, and will be, with the earth that was, and will not be; the light of heaven, where they need no candle, neither light of the sun, with the luminaries of earth, subject to extinction; the appearance of the glorified, compared with the sinful children of Adam; the *lingering traces*, it may be, and *faint resemblance*, it may be, in the *form* and *features* of those whom they meet in heaven, with what their friends *were* when they left them.

The question has been put, Does the disembodied soul of the glorified retain something of the form and the features of the body in which it once dwelt? Angels have *form* and *feature*. Souls disembodied *must* have such attributes; and it may be that it is the *features* of the soul shining in and through the features of the body that we behold when we look into the face of a friend: for look upon the same countenance after death; and, oh, what a change! — so changed, to use a mean figure, as the face of the lantern is when the candle is blown out. Whilst the candle burns within, is it not *its* form and appearance, and not those of the lantern merely, that you saw when you looked upon it and enjoyed its light?

It seems to be the same with the soul and body of man. The soul, in its disembodied and glorified state, *may* assuredly retain something, for any thing to the contrary known to us, of the form and features of the body which it once inhabited. The child bears a resemblance to the parent. It may be, that through this, and in this way, the glorified who are in heaven may come, in the exercise of their *judgment* and *observation*, to *recognize* their friends when they meet them there, changed, glorified, beautified though they be, compared with what they were when they last looked upon them in the world.

There is not merely a *something* in each individual member of the human family which constitutes *identity:* there is a something also which constitutes *personality*, or *individuality*. It has been observed, that amongst the millions and millions of the human family who have appeared successively upon earth, two persons have not been found whose countenances have been in every respect *exactly* alike: each has a *peculiarity* and an *individuality* of aspect; and it is only trite to say, it is *this* infinite variety that enables us to distinguish the one from the other.

This personality of aspect, and individuality of appearance, continue to exist during the various changes through which an individual passes from childhood to youth, and from youth to old age. The individual changes in size, and also in appearance; but, in the midst of these mutations, there is a *something* peculiar retained, which never altogether disappears.

For any thing that we can tell, this *peculiarity* of the form, expression, and aspect of the countenance, may *continue* for ever: indeed, analogy is in favor of the supposition. What efforts do we make to discover a missing relative! and do we not persevere until we generally succeed? Paul, as we have said, succeeded in discovering Onesimus in the great and crowded city of Rome, then the metropolis of the world. Will ye, after a search made *through all eternity*, not succeed in discovering your friends in the metropolis of the universe? The mystic spouse went into the midst of the city in search of Him whom her soul loved. She went up and down its crowded streets. She inquired at the watchman for her Beloved. She used all the means that were within her reach to discover him, until at last she met him: then, with a heart glowing in love, she held him, and would not let him go. And will ye wander in sad disappointment for ever through the streets of the heavenly Jerusalem, and inquire at all the glorified whom you meet, and will your search for them be all in vain? The aspirations of the spirit say, "No."

Some years ago, a boy, four years of age, disappeared one day whilst playing at a little distance from his parents' door. The most diligent search was made by the police, by the distracted parents, and by their friends, for the little strayed wanderer; but it was all in vain. Upwards of two years after, the father of the boy happened, by mere accident, to turn into the police-office whilst passing it, merely to look in idle curiosity at what was transacting there, and to loiter away a few minutes which he had at his disposal. When he entered, the magistrate upon the bench had just passed sentence of imprisonment against a woman who had been found guilty of theft. She was still seated at the bar, and a little boy was standing at her side. The moment the father saw the boy, he recognized him; and, with a burst of joyous distraction, he cried out, "My child!" flew towards him, and clasped him in his arms. The boy knew his father, and, recoiling from the woman, clung to him. The woman, however, stoutly and impudently maintained that the boy was her own son. The father appealed to the scar of a burn under the boy's arm, in proof of the truth of his assertion. When the boy was stripped, the scar was *there*.

Angels probably have, in the midst of the resplendent sameness of their forms, this complexional dissimilarity, this individuality of aspect, and personality of appearance. When the unfallen angels meet the fallen, whom they knew and with whom they once associated in heaven, do they not know them and recognize them as *old* companions, though their countenances doubtless are changed, — dark, scowling, and degraded? I believe the glorified retain, to some extent at least, the *individuality* of aspect which they once possessed upon earth; and by this they will be known and distinguished by their respective *names* and *forms* for ever.

We are not entitled to suppose that God the Father will not discover our friends to us when we come to stand before him in glory; that Jesus our Saviour will not say in those high courts what he said to the Apostle John, as he stood at the foot of the cross, "Behold thy mother!" that the Holy Spirit will not impart to us an intuitive knowledge of our friends, and, by an internal impulse upon our souls, bring us to their presence, that we may recognize them and discourse with them; that angels will not reveal to us *where* our mothers or fathers, sisters or brothers, sons or daughters, are; that none of the glorified will listen to our inquiries. But, even under such an extravagant assumption, can it be denied, that I may succeed myself, by virtue of an intuition not altogether independent of a scrutiny, aided by memory and intelligence?

Again: God's children enter heaven in possession of all their social affections. This proves recognition. God gives us no part either of our corporeal or mental or moral or social constitution in vain. We know he has implanted in our bosoms a *longing* after immortality, a *dread* and *recoil* at the very thought of annihilation. So has he provided the province for the realization of this holy aspiration, in the gift of eternal life through Jesus Christ our Lord.

Christianity does not only not destroy the social affections of our nature: it ennobles and purifies them. Grace is not given to eradicate this part of our moral constitution, but to etherealize it; and in the recognition of our friends in heaven, and in the loving intercourse that awaits us there with them, God has provided *one* province for the development of these social affections on and on without end.

CHAPTER V.

RECOGNITION OF FRIENDS IN HEAVEN (*continued*).

PROOF SEVENTH. — FRIENDS MEET IN HEAVEN AFTER HAVING ASSOCIATED FOR A SEASON UPON EARTH: THIS FACT MUST SECURE THEIR RECOGNITION.

OD'S children do not meet in heaven as children meet in a home, who, born successively into the same family, meet for the *first* time: they meet for the second time. It may not be deemed beneath the dignity and reverence of our subject if we allude to an Eastern fable: It happened that a certain soul was destined to inhabit, for a time, the body of a dove; another, that of a swallow; and another, that of a lark. In that pre-existent state, they lived in the same cage,—with liberty, however, to roam about wherever they chose,—and formed plans for taking excursions in company to and fro through the earth, and over the sea, and up over the cliffs of lofty mountains; and then spread their wings, and away, away, over out-stretching valleys with their green, grassy sward,

and over woods vocal with their feathery songsters; and experienced in each other's company numberless adventures, such as doves and swallows and larks are subject to. But the time came, when, upon the principle of the doctrine of the transmigration of souls, they were to be born and numbered among the members of the human family. The soul of the dove passed into a child; that of the swallow, into the brother of that child; and that of the lark, into a sister of these two; there being two years between the births. They were successively born in the same parents' home, with a full recollection of the past, and, of course, with their intellectual faculties such as those of other human beings. They did not at first know each other as having been prior companions; but, when they grew up, they began to speak about the past, and about the events that had occurred to them during the life they had led as birds, before they became numbered with human beings. They spoke about their former cage, contrasting it with the home they had entered, and about their flights with swallows to Africa; with other doves to the high mountain-tops; with singing larks, as they went whirring up, on the mornings of many glad summers, to the very gates of heaven. They spoke about their narrow escapes from the prowling sportsman, and the lower animals with which they accidently came into contact, whilst skimming the air in their flights together; nor was it long ere they came to be satisfied that they had met before, and had lived together, and had talked before in their own way, as doves and swallows and larks talk, and had taken frequent flights in each other's company. They thus became great lovers of each other: and then it was raised among them as a question, whether the one life was better than the other; but they all came to one conclusion. One feared the sportsman's gun, another the fowler's snare, and the third the cruel hawk; and they resolved that it was better to be human creatures than birds.

This simple fable may form the lowlier term of a contrast, the other term of which is so much more grand, we should say rather, sublime; but there is also in it—which is no contradiction—a similitude. If we consider the vast difference in the capacity and sensibility of the higher creature, as compared with that of the lower, we arrive at the so much greater certainty, that the thoughts and sympathies of the earth-born mind must be the prelude and occasion of that recognition among the glorified, which is so dear to our hopes, that we cannot even bear to have it called in question.

CHAPTER VI.

RECOGNITION OF FRIENDS IN HEAVEN (*continued*).

PROOF EIGHTH. — THE JUDGMENT-DAY WILL INEVITABLY SECURE THE RECOGNITION OF FRIENDS.

EVEN if it *be possible* that friends who meet in heaven do not discover each other before, the judgment will make the discovery. "Behold, the Lord cometh with ten thousand of his saints to execute judgment upon all." "Behold, He cometh with clouds, and every eye shall see him, and they also which pierced him; and all kindreds of the earth shall wail because of him." "I beheld till the thrones were cast down, and the Ancient of days did sit, whose garment was white as snow, and the hair of his head like the pure wool: his throne was like the fiery flame, and his wheels as burning fire. A fiery stream issued and came forth from before him; thousand thousands ministered unto him, and ten thousand times ten thousand stood before him: the judgment was set, and the books were opened." "And I saw a great white throne, and

Him that sat on it, from whose face the earth and the heaven fled away; and there was found no place for them. And I saw the dead, small and great, stand before God; and the books were opened; and another book was opened, which is the book of life; and the dead were judged out of those things which were written in the books, according to their works."

TWO OPPOSITE VIEWS OF CHRIST'S PROCEDURE AT THE JUDGMENT.

There are two opposite views which Christians have adopted respecting the mode of *procedure* which Christ will adopt in judging the members of the human family. One view is, that there will be no such thing as a *personal* and *individual* judgment at all, and no *exposure* of every person's name and life before the mighty hosts of the assembled universe. According to this view, the *procedure* of the judgment-day is set forth: The heavens over the earth will rend asunder; the gates of glory will be thrown open; the everlasting doors will be lifted up; the Lord Jesus Christ will be seen by all the assembled hosts rising in his glory from the right hand of the throne of God, about to descend for the judgment of the world. The whole inhabitants of heaven will instantly be in motion; angels, the spirits of the just made perfect, about to receive their bodies raised by the Lord from the grave. Enoch and Elijah, in their already glorified bodies, will follow in the Redeemer's train, heaven will be emptied for a little space of all its created inhabitants, and silence will reign for a season in its previously crowded and vocal courts. The Lord Jesus will burst upon the view of the startled nations with all the mighty hosts around him. He will appear in his own glory, in the glory of the Father, and in the glory of all his holy angels. The Lord Jesus left the world, at his ascension to heaven, seated upon the bosom of a white cloud. He is about, in bodily presence, to revisit the world, seated upon the great white throne. He shall come, not with the roll of silver trumpets sounding forth the announcement that the jubilee is come to the prisoners in Palestine, but with the trump of God proclaiming that an eternal jubilee has come to the prisoners of the grave. For the moment the glad sound of that trump is heard, the dead shall rise. All who are in the grave shall hear his voice, and shall come forth. Thus, in a moment, in the twinkling of an eye, there will be seen one rising, moving, wide-spread mass gathering themselves together, numerous as the sands of the sea, from the east and from the west, from the north and from the south, even from the four winds of heaven; to all, the judgment-throne the centre of attraction.

When the Lord Jesus takes his seat, some think that he will simply separate the righteous from the wicked into two great throngs. The righteous shall assemble and gather together, and in one rejoicing mass take their position at once on the Judge's right hand. The wicked will, at the same moment, move on from their graves, and take their position at the Judge's left hand, a mighty mass of trembling criminals, with countenances black with despair, the glare of whose fright-speaking eyes will show that all hope has for ever fled. The Judge turns his face towards those at his right hand, and addresses them: "Come, ye blessed of my Father, inherit the kingdom prepared for you from the foundation of the world." Then, turning to those on his left hand: "Depart from me, ye cursed, into everlasting fire, prepared for the devil and his angels." The righteous will then instantly rise with singing and gladness, and will follow the Lord of glory upwards, and enter into heaven. The wicked will at the same time, with failing and throbbing hearts, take the last look of the rising and ascending assemblage; and, in the hearing of the burst of praise that is rolling down from heaven, they will depart to the punishment that awaits them.

According to this view, the whole procedure of the judgment-day will not occupy more than a few minutes, or a few hours at most; for, the moment the sentence is pronounced, the two assemblages on the right and left hands of the Judge will go at once to enter their appointed but very different dwellings.

If this view of the *procedure* of the last day be correct, friends *may* meet at the judgment-throne, and not recognize each other; because there is thus to be no *individual exposure* and *personal judgment*, so as to *proclaim* the *name*, and to *exhibit* the *life*, and to *expose* the *past conduct* and *actings*, of the person judged. Those who have adopted this view found their opinion chiefly upon the Scripture descriptions of it given in the twenty-fifth chapter of Matthew's Gospel. But we should remember that the view which St. Matthew gives of the judgment-day is simply, that there will then, and not *till* then, be an entire separation of the wicked from amongst the righteous; but he does *not* delineate there the *procedure* which the Judge will observe in the trial of those before him. I remark, too, that the view now given involves the assumption, that there will be a trial of those merely who shall be living upon the earth at the last day. All the rest of the human family — according to our Protestant interpretation, that the souls of God's people at their death pass immediately to glory, whilst the souls of the wicked go at once to punishment — were separated before.

I believe, however, that the judgment of the great day will be a very *different process* from that which those who hold this view imagine. There is, accordingly, *another view* held by devout Christians, and which I believe to be the correct and scriptural one, — that *every member* of the human family will undergo a *personal*, an *individual*, and an *accurate scrutinizing judgment* and *exposure*, in the *presence* of the *assembled universe*.

The great Judge is not merely to separate the righteous from the wicked as a shepherd divideth his sheep from the goats: *the Books are to be opened*,— the Book of God's Omniscience, the Book of God's Providence with each individual, the Book of Conscience. The opening of these books will show to the whole vast assemblages the *principle* of *justice* with *mercy*, upon which the righteous are acquitted; and that of *justice* without mercy, upon which the wicked are condemned.

Every believer and sinner, then, may now say this with himself: "I will be judged as minutely as if Christ had come down from heaven, and the judgment had been appointed to sit for *my trial alone*. My whole life will be passed in review by Christ, before the assembled universe: every action I have performed, every word I have spoken, every thought that has passed through my mind, will be taken cognizance of on that great and terrible day."

This, reader, is the nature of the judgment that awaiteth thee. Prepare for it now! Live above the world! Live to God! Live for eternity! Walk in Jesus! Thou art compassed about, even now, by a great cloud of witnesses, both in heaven and upon earth. Thou wilt be compassed at the judgment-throne by a greater assembly. Therefore lay aside every weight and thy besetting sin; run with patience the race that God has set before thee, ever looking to Jesus as thy only rescue.

According to this view of the *procedure* at the judgment-day, friends will *recognize* each other there; for their *names* will be announced before each other, and their *intercourse* will be passed in review. Nay, their thoughts about their friends, their words addressed to their friends, their actions performed to or by their friends, constitute the greater part of their life. The Holy Spirit evidently gives us this startling view of the *particularity* of the great and last review. "Let us hear the conclusion of the whole matter: Fear God, and keep his commandments; for this is the whole duty of man. For God shall *bring every work* into judgment, with *every secret thing*, whether it be good, or whether it be evil." "For we must all appear before the judgment-seat of Christ, that every one may *receive* the *things done* in his body, according to that he *hath* done, whether it be good or bad." We have already seen, that Paul looks forward to the judgment-throne with the anticipation that he will meet his Thessalonian converts there, and recognize them there, and experience them to be his crown of joy and of rejoicing. If Paul will recognize these Thessalonians, when their intercourse and acts of friendship are revealed, will you not recognize your friends, with whom you have associated, when your intercourse is passed in review? You will meet your friends at the judgment-throne; that is certain:

the *way* in which you have lived together, and acted towards each other, will be *reviewed.* That review will afford the evidence to the great assize, that the Judge is proceeding upon the principles of infinite justice and equity, either in your acquittal or condemnation.

There stands in Christ's glorious presence a father, joyful and glad, in the front of the great white throne. His children are beside him, and they are now to him a crown of joy and of rejoicing; for that man was not merely the natural father of these children, but their spiritual father also. He labored in their behalf, not merely for the bread that perisheth; but he wrestled in prayer, at the footstool of God's throne of grace, for their salvation, and earnestly entreated his Father in heaven to bestow upon his dearly-beloved children the bread of life, — the spiritual manna from heaven, — that they might eat thereof, and never die. His labor was not in vain. By his holy example, by his heavenly conversation, by his prayers for them, so full of a holy unction and of a holy earnestness, nay, so full of Christ, and of the very breathings of his love, he yearned and longed and travailed that Christ might be formed in their souls the hope of glory. His desire was granted; his prayers were answered; and there these children stand in the presence of him who was *once* their father; and *there* he appears before Jesus, able to say, both in a *natural* and *spiritual* sense, "Here am I, and the children whom thou hast given me." If that father and these children know each other at the judgment-bar, — and it is not possible that their intercourse can be publicly reviewed, and their pious conduct towards each other publicly exhibited to their praise, and as the *reason* why they are accepted, whilst other families are cast out and condemned, without becoming known to each other, — will they lose this recognition of each other after they rise and enter heaven, to associate there as the members of the same family for ever?

There stands another father before the great white throne, with his face displaying his agonies, and his mouth the chokings of despair; and there his poor children are quaking in horror beside him. Their fear and trembling are not without a cause. That father was a drunkard; he was a deserter from Christian ordinances; he gave himself up to a life of dissipation and of ungodliness; he never prayed; he never read the Bible; he never went to church; he never spoke to his children about God, about Jesus, about the coming judgment-day, about heaven, about hell, about the great realities of the eternal world, about the necessity and the urgency of seeking by prayer from God the salvation of their souls. He succeeded but too well in effecting the ruin of his children; not that he wished it, but his example and his whole conduct were exactly such as were unfailingly calculated to effect their damnation. That father was not a ministering angel for Christ in earnestly endeavoring to secure his children's salvation: he was an agent for Satan in effecting their ruin. He died impenitent. His children grew up, walked in the footsteps of their ungodly father, died also in a state of alienation from God, and were lost. Now they are met for judgment in the presence of Christ; but, alas! it is as mutual accusers. The father shrinks back and trembles at the sight of his poor lost children, standing in their agony before him. Think ye there will be no recognition there?

I make a solemn appeal to the consciences of all who may read these pages. Remember, your present life will be passed in review before the assembled universe. Do not imagine that you will pass in the crowd almost unnoticed. On the great and terrible day of the Lord, the book of your present life will be opened and read, whilst a listening universe is looking on. That book will not be a *flattering* and *high-colored memoir;* a false and unfounded eulogy, representing more what your life *should* have been, than what it really *was:* it will be a full, an accurate, and a truthful revelation of all that you have *thought* and *said* and *done, as if your moral image were reflected in the clear, undimmed glass of eternal truth.*

CHAPTER VII.

OBJECTIONS ANSWERED.

HERE are four objections which may be brought against the views which I have advanced.

OBJECTION FIRST.

The resurrection-body will be so entirely different from what it is now, that friends will be unable to recognize each other when they meet at the judgment-throne.

This objection may be stated in a familiar way, thus: As the butterfly sporting on a summer day has little, if any, resemblance to the grub that slept wingless and motionless only a little while before among the clods of the valley; so the glorified body will be so changed and improved, that all traces of what it was once will have vanished, and consequently a *recognition* and *identification* of friends will be impossible.

ANSWER.

I have already obviated this objection so far, by referring to the *continuity* of *aspect*, *personality* of *form*, and *similarity* of *features*, which the body retains during life in the midst of the changes (and they are many and great) through which it passes from infancy to youth, from youth to manhood, and from manhood to old age. For any thing I can tell, this *continuity* of *form* and *feature* through life may be a *premonition* of what the body of every individual is to be after translation. Nay, I understand that naturalists assert that the winged insect does retain much of the form and characteristics which it had whilst a grub.

There are *several errors*, in their *religious views*, into which individuals are too apt to fall: 1st, Imagining that there is a greater difference than what really exists betwixt a state of *nature* and a state of *grace;* 2d, Betwixt a state of *grace* here and a state of *glory* in heaven; and, 3d, Betwixt what the body is *now*, whilst in a state of *health* and of *youth*, and what it is to *become* when it receives its *resurrection-form* and *glory*.

There are individuals who think that a state of *grace* is so different from a state of *nature*, that the moment you are born again, and become, through the gracious operations of the Holy Spirit upon your souls, the new creation of God in Christ Jesus, you cease to be yourselves; the whole form and features of your souls are so changed, that you are, in fact, no longer the persons that you were before. What does God's grace do to the soul? It imparts to it a new *bias*, a Godward and a heavenward tendency; but it neither imparts to the convert a *new* spirit, nor a spirit so changed that it retains none of the features which it exhibited before.

The breath of spring does not create a *new* earth, but throws into the old soil such a vivifying influence as to cause the grass to grow, the flowers to appear, the crops to spring up, and the birds to sing among the foliaged branches of the trees. Paul has zeal before his conversion: he retains his zeal after it. Peter was forward and outspoken before his regeneration: he is the same in this respect after.

Again: there are those who think that a state of *glory* in heaven is so very different from a state of *grace* upon earth, that, the moment we enter the world of glory, we will *cease* to be ourselves; we will be lost, and swallowed up, and absorbed, if not in God, at least in the contemplation of his glory. For any thing I can tell (and analogy lends its countenance to the supposition), whilst Newton in heaven finds his chief enjoyment in communion with God, he may still be engaged in the contemplation and study of astronomy; and now a universe in extent and grandeur and beauty may be expanded around him, and may be the object of his enraptured gaze, of which he had no conception whatever whilst in this world. I do not believe, that, in a state of *glory*, we are to be so very different from what we are *now* in a state of *grace*, that we will actually not be the same persons; that we will cease to be ourselves. *Glory is grace in the flower; grace is glory in the bud.*

There is a *similar* error committed by many individuals respecting the *extent* of the change which the body is to undergo at the resurrection. Indeed, according to the views of some, the body of the glorified will be so very different, not from what it was when laid in the grave, but from what it was during life, that it will not be the same body in any respect, and consequently will thus retain nothing of its former form and features and appearance. This is a special error. The Scriptures countenance the doctrine, that, when the body has become glorified, this corruptible shall put on incorruption, and this mortal shall put on immortality, when we hear the trump of God and the stir of the resurrection-morning in our deep, dark prison; and when we come up out of it, and take our stand at the judgment-throne of Christ, wearing and exhibiting in our upraised bodies the very image of Jesus, we will be both changed and improved: but it does not follow that we will *cease* to be ourselves, and that we will retain *no trace* of our own *peculiar aspect;* that we shall have *lost for ever* that which constituted previously our peculiar *personality* and *individuality*. Yes, the very same body is to be raised by Christ, to become the tabernacle and dwelling-place of the soul for ever; or otherwise that body is not to undergo a *resurrection* merely on that great day, but there is to be a *new creation.*

Again: the greatness of the change, according to the opinion of some, would be tantamount to our not being the same creatures. It is here forgotten, that, after Christ's resurrection, his body was not *so* changed that his disciples and followers did not know him. They *recognized* him, and beheld, in his continued *resemblance* to what he *was before* he went down into the tomb, that it was he himself. They knew the tones of his voice; they recognized his very *form* and his very *features*. They beheld the marks of the nails in his feet and in his hands, and the gash of the spear in his side.

OBJECTION SECOND.

The lives of God's people will not be exposed by Christ at the judgment-throne, and before an assembled universe, so as to make them known to each other by a full exhibition both of their good actions and also of their sins; for the following passages of Scripture *seem to teach the doctrine*, that when their sins are sought for they will not be found, but will be cast into the depths of the sea, will have passed into oblivion, and consequently will not be exposed or known: "In those days, and in that time, saith the Lord, the iniquity of Israel shall be sought for, and there shall be none; and the sins of Judah, and they shall not be found: for I will pardon them whom I reserve." "Who is a God like unto thee, that pardoneth iniquity, and passeth by the transgression of the remnant of his heritage? He retaineth not his anger for ever, because he delighteth in mercy. He will turn again; he will have compassion upon us; he will subdue our iniquities; and thou wilt cast all their sins into the depths of the sea." "Thou hast in love to my soul delivered it from the pit of corruption; for thou hast cast all my sins behind thy back."

ANSWER.

These passages of Scripture merely teach, that, through the blood of Christ, the sins of God's people will be fully *remitted* and *blotted out*, and will be so *completely forgiven and removed*, as if cast by God himself behind his back, and flung into the depths of the sea. But these passages *do* not and *cannot* prove that their sins will be hidden from the assembled universe, and consequently that their lives will not be fully and faithfully exhibited and made known, and thus afford the opportunity to their friends of recognizing them, for the following reasons: —

1. *The Scriptures elsewhere teach the very contrary*, in language in which there is no metaphor. "God will bring *every work* into judgment, with *every secret thing*." "For there is nothing *hid* which shall not be *manifested*." "I say unto you, that every idle word that men shall speak, they shall give account thereof in the day of judgment."

2. *The very object, the grand design, of the judgment-day, is to make such a full and particular exposure of the lives both of the righteous and of the wicked, that the Lord Jesus may prove to the satisfaction of the intelligent universe assembled around him, as the great, the last, and the grand jury, that he is just, and is acting justly, both when he acquits and when he condemns.* This object can only be gained by a full exposure of the whole lives of each, even to the minutest particularity.

3. *It is only a full exposure of the lives of God's people, their sins set in array before the assembled universe, that will exalt Christ sufficiently, and bear suitable evidence to the infinite efficacy of the blood of Immanuel, and to the great and unspeakable benefits that result to his people through faith in his blood.*

Thus the exposure of the sins of God's people at the judgment-throne will be the means of *magnifying Christ* before all who shall be there, and of showing *how much* believers owe to Jesus; for, numerous and aggravated as their sins have been, — evidenced by the exposure of them, — Christ's blood has washed them all away.

God's people do not conceal their sins from God during their life: they confess them in prayer to their Father in heaven. God's people, moreover, who have already entered heaven, do not conceal their sins. They do not pretend, yonder, that they never had any; for thus they sing of the blood of Christ in the courts of eternal glory: "Unto Him that loved us, and washed us from our *sins* in his own blood, and hath made us kings and priests unto God and his Father; to Him be glory and dominion for ever and ever." "Thou wast slain, and hast *redeemed* us to God, by thy *blood*, out of every kindred and tongue and people and nation." Will, then, the sins of God's people be concealed and hidden, and never be referred to, at the judgment-throne? Were this really to be done, Christ would there be robbed of half his glory, because the righteous might be looked upon as acquitted and saved, *because* in their lives they had been righteous and holy, and not *because*, through faith, they had washed their robes, and made them white in the blood of the Lamb.

4. If the sins of God's people are not exposed at the judgment-throne, that the Lord Jesus may receive the glory due to his name in washing them all away through the efficacy of his shed blood, *then a monstrous injustice has been done by the Holy Spirit, in the descriptions of the Bible, to David, and to the rest of the children of God, whose sins are particularly, and with considerable circumstantiality of detail, mentioned in the Holy Scriptures.* The drunkenness of Noah, the drunkenness and incest of Lot, the falsehood of Abraham, the duplicity of Jacob, the deceit of Joseph, the lies and oaths and curses of Peter, the whole apostles deserting their Lord, the blasphemies and persecutions of Paul, and, above all, the sins of

adultery and murder which David committed in the days of his sad aberration, are all particularly promulgated.

Wherever the Bible has been circulated, the sins of murder and adultery committed by David have been particularly noticed. Consequently, all who have gone up to heaven at death have entered it with the full knowledge of these two dark and terrible sins; and thus, when one enters heaven and looks upon David, he will, by the mental law of association, recall the account which he has read in the Book of Life.

Nor can we forget that it would only put all God's children upon an *equality* with David, and with the others whose sins are mentioned in the Bible, were *their* sins also exposed and *revealed* at the judgment-throne, and this not to their *shame* and *confusion of face*, but for the *magnifying* of the *grace of Jesus*. Would it exhibit an impartial display of God's dealings with his children, that David's sins, and the sins of the rest of God's children whose names are so mentioned, should be so universally known, both by all God's translated children and by those also who are still living upon the earth, and that the sins of all others should be hid? Rest assured that God's dealings with his children will not be so unequal and so partial. In the *exposure* which the Scriptures have *already* made, there is the *foreshadowing intimation* given of the fuller exposure that will *yet* be made, when the necessities of judgment call for the revelation.

And thus we have the lesson: Do not dream, people of God, that your sins will be hidden at the judgment-throne, but live *now* so holily and circumspectly, through the exercise of a living faith upon the Son of God, that your sins then to be exposed may be *few*, and that your good works may be *many*.

OBJECTION THIRD.

The remembrance of our sins, in heaven, which we committed upon earth, would impair our happiness there; and consequently we cannot carry up with us into heaven a full remembrance of the past.

ANSWER.

The remembrance in heaven of the sins committed upon earth will not act upbraidingly upon the spirit; will not be the dark and lingering shadows of remorse, overclouding and distressing our glorified and enraptured spirit; but will bring up to us through eternity our obligations to God's eternal love, and to the unspeakable riches of his grace, that has conferred upon *us*, once so sinful and all undeserving, the salvation of our soul: it will bring up to us, and that for ever, *what* we owe to Jesus and to his shed blood, and *how much* we should love Him who has loved us, even with an everlasting love, — a love that many waters could not quench, and that many floods could not drown.

Nay, the remembrance of our sins, in heaven, which

we committed upon earth, great and aggravated, and all washed away through the blood of Jesus, will rather be as oil to the flame of our love. Thus we will be led to sing of Jesus, — a song that will appear to us to be always new, — whilst the joyful cycles of a glad eternity are rolling over us: "Thou wast slain, and hast redeemed us to God, by thy blood, out of every kindred and tongue and people and nation."

We cannot suppose David feels heaven's happiness to be lessened in his experience, because, in the midst of its glories, he remembers the sins which he committed whilst he remained upon earth; nor that the sight of Bathsheba beside him in heaven — if she be there — will bring in his recollections a cloud over its sky; a gloom, and something like a sombre and sorrowful night, over its scenery. No: rather that he uses the remembrance of his sins to increase his love to Him as "the morning-star," whose rising upon his soul, whilst benighted through his transgressions, dispelled the darkness of remorse, and brought back to him the dawn of a joyful day.

You will not merely remember your sins in heaven: you will remember also all that you did for Christ whilst in the world.

This remembrance will show you the gain the glorified have acquired by entering among the blessed, and the troubles they have escaped by being away from earth; yea, it will add fervor to your devotion, and a depth of holier earnestness to your songs of praise. Just as the *remembrance* of the dangers which the pilgrim has escaped, whilst in his travels through foreign lands, enhances in his estimation the comfort of his home; so the *recollection* of earth, with its checkered scenes, its sorrows, its trials, its tears, its death, forms a contrast with joys that to us are inexpressible. Rest is sweet after toil; health, after sickness; freedom, after slavery; joy, after sorrow; life, after death; heaven, after earth.

The souls of the martyrs under the altar in heaven remember the sins of their enemies. "How long," is their cry, "O Lord, holy and true, dost thou not judge and avenge our blood on them that dwell on the earth?" Do these martyrs now remember the sins of their enemies, and have they forgotten their own? It cannot be! Every song which the saved sing before the throne of God in heaven, giving honor and thanksgiving and praise to Him who is upon it, will be enhanced by the recollection, "Thou wast slain, and hast redeemed us to God by thy blood." "Worthy is the Lamb that was slain, to receive power and riches and wisdom and strength and honor and glory and blessing."

OBJECTION FOURTH.

The recognition of our friends in heaven will become a source of sorrow to us there, when we thus discover that some beloved one is not there beside us, but is lost.

This objection may be stated also thus: A mother is saved, and at her death she ascends among the blessed. She finds, through the privilege she has of recognizing her former friends, that her once dearly-beloved child, who died before her, is not there. Will this knowledge not impair and lessen, if it does not destroy for ever, that mother's happiness?

ANSWER.

The Lord Jesus Christ is the key to solve all these difficulties, conjured up by a fruitful imagination. The objection *assumes*, that it is the *greatness* of the mother's love to her child, and her *knowledge* she has gained since she entered heaven that her child is lost, that takes away her own happiness there. I ask the objector this question: Does the Lord Jesus Christ love that mother's child *less* than she does? and does he not know this irreparable loss? If so, does this knowledge *destroy Christ's* joy and happiness in heaven? Besides, I address myself further to the objector. You *deny* the doctrine that we will know our translated friends, or that there will be any *recognition* whatever, which I have endeavored to prove, and in which I firmly believe; and you advance a mere *supposition* against the doctrine, as if it were an *argument establishing* the *opposite* of that doctrine: for you *suppose*, that, if the general position be true, the mother in heaven, who knows that her child is not there, will become, if not absolutely miserable, at least less happy, where all is represented as joyful.

But suppose, for the sake of argument, the *contrary* doctrine true, that the mother does *not recognize* any of her former friends, and consequently does *not* recognize her own once-beloved child among the saved, even whilst her child, it is certain, *is* there: then, in that case, her child is *lost* to her. According to your view, she has not the means of knowing that her child really *is* saved; and thus, if she be capable of reflection, she will be in a state of uncertainty for ever as regards a fact as important to her as her own salvation. Yes, if your objection be valid, — but, thanks be to God, it is not so, — then all who are in heaven will suffer the *misery* of *not* knowing whether or not dear friends, who once walked with them in the ways of God upon earth, *are* among the blessed, and are, along with them, forming a portion of God's great family, — the inmates with them, for eternity, of the same happy home.

By robbing heaven of the *social aspect*, in which the Scriptures set it before us as our home, in which we are to meet with those we loved, and *recognize* them amid the light of eternity, you are plucking from the crown, which we are to wear for ever, one of its brightest gems; you are taking away one sun of comfort that will shine upon us from its high firmament; you are drying up one river of holy joy, that will flow and reflow through the souls of friends, when they meet each other in their Father's home, and know even as also they are known.

> "A few short years of evil past,
> We reach the happy shore,
> Where death-divided friends at last
> Shall meet to part no more."

PART III.

The Interest those in Heaven feel in Earth.

"LIKEWISE JOY SHALL BE IN HEAVEN OVER ONE SINNER THAT REPENTETH."

CHAPTER I.

THE INTEREST THOSE IN HEAVEN FEEL IN EARTH.

WHETHER or not those in heaven feel an interest in us who are still upon the earth, is not a subject of mere idle speculation. The belief that they *do* is calculated to exert a powerful influence upon us in relation to our life and conduct in the world; but, in order that this influence may be exerted, we must realize and carry about the thought of it abidingly with us.

The child at school, on the examination-day, feels stimulated to exert himself to the utmost, that he may acquit himself well when he beholds his parents and other visitors present, fixing their eyes upon him, and deeply interested in his success. David felt animated whilst advancing to engage in single combat with Goliath, not only by the view that he was meeting his antagonist under the protection and shield of the God of sabaoth, but also by the thought that Saul, King of Israel, and the whole Jewish troops, on the one side, and the Philistine battalions, on the other, were looking on, deeply interested spectators, and were, with trembling anxiety, watching the issue of the meeting of the two very unequal combatants. The servant feels an additional motive to use diligence in his work, when he beholds his master by his side looking on, and his fellow-servants also spectators of his activity or idleness. The competitor at the Olympic games felt himself animated and stimulated to put forth his utmost exertion, and to strain every nerve, that he might outstrip his fellow-competitors, and win the crown, when he looked to the end of the race-course, and saw the judge of the games sitting there with his eyes fastened upon him, and again looked upon each side of the arena, and saw there congregated around him the great crowd of spectators, collected from the surrounding countries, with their forests of heads all bent forward in eagerness, and watching all breathlessly his progress towards the goal.

We may suppose what would be the effect upon *us*, who are now in the world, competitors for a crown of glory that is never to fade, if we saw the omniscient eye of Father, Son, and Holy Ghost, constantly looking out from heaven upon us by day, as visibly as we see the sun in his meridian splendor, and observe the eyes of angels and of the glorified fixed upon us by night, with a brilliancy equal to that of the stars looking out upon us from their quiet, far-off homes, in the clear, frosty night. Surely the view of the great heavenly assembly looking on, and witnesses of what we are doing (and yet all this is being done, though we do not see it), would lead us to lay aside every weight, and the sin which doth so easily beset us, and to run with patience the race that is set before us.

Yes, the men of the world who have not that faith which is the substance of things hoped for, and the evidence of things not seen, behold no such sight above them as this assemblage of spectators; they hear not the roll of the applauding multitudes in the skies; and thus the thought, that those in the heavens feel a deep interest in us, scarcely ever enters their mind.

The men of the world have but a dreamy view of heaven and its inhabitants; so dim and visionary and shadowy, that they can scarcely be said to have realized their existence at all. To speak to such worldlings about the *interest* which those in heaven feel in the inhabitants of the earth, is to talk to them in an unknown tongue. Even Christians have generally but vague conceptions of heaven, and those who dwell in it. *They* believe in the *existence* of heaven, it is true; but it can scarcely be said that ever they *realize* it. Even in the view of many believers, heaven is more a *name* than a *home;* it is more a flitting, unsubstantial *vision*, than a *world*,—the dwelling-place of the glorified.

I wish to remind such individuals, that heaven exists as truly as the earth does; that there are as truly members constituting the family of God there, living, active, reflective, interested, not in what is taking place among themselves merely, but in every act, thought, and feeling in the human race, as there are members constituting *your* family circle, and who feel interested, more or less, in what is occurring within your limited sphere. Nor are you to imagine that *space* or *time* have any thing to do with this question. Look at the various mechanical contrivances of our day which have been the means of bringing the people of distant nations near to each other. Not only are the inhabitants of the earth better known to each other: they now feel far more interest in what is going on in every part of its surface than they did some hundred years ago. It *may* be that this increase of interest is just a visible symbol, but still a cold and feeble representation, of that interest which the inhabitants of heaven feel in all that is going on throughout the whole wide and boundless domains of God's great universe.

The Scriptures alone can determine this question: *What* is the *degree* and the *extent* of this *interest?* Accordingly, it is the announcements made in the word of God upon which we must *chiefly* rest. Yet, even if the Scriptures had been altogether silent upon the subject, there are some considerations, constituting what may be termed the *philosophical argument*, which must naturally lead us to infer, not only the existence of that interest, but also its degree.

PHILOSOPHICAL EVIDENCES FOR THIS INTEREST.

Reason's Proofs in favor of the *supposition*, that *those* who are in *heaven must* feel an interest in *us* who are dwelling upon the *earth.*

1. *The same God presides over both worlds.*

God created, he also *reigns* over, both heaven and earth. "The Lord hath established his throne in the heavens, and his kingdom ruleth over all." "Heaven is God's throne: the earth is his footstool." "And I heard as it were the voice of a great multitude, and as the voice of many waters, and as the voice of mighty thunderings, saying, Alleluia; for the Lord God omnipotent reigneth." "I blessed the Most High, and I praised and honored Him that liveth for ever, whose dominion is an everlasting dominion, and his kingdom is from generation to generation. And all the inhabitants of the earth are reputed as nothing; and he doeth according to his will in the army of heaven, and among the inhabitants of the earth; and none can stay his hand, or say unto him, What doest thou?"

The inhabitants of earth feel an interest in what is going on in heaven. I pass over here (of course) the *interest* which the inspired penmen show, everywhere in their writings, that they felt for this land of promise to the redeemed, and simply appeal to *your thoughts* about heaven who read these pages, and to *your inevitable musings* in all hours about what may be going on there. It cannot be but that you feel an interest in a future state, because you cannot avoid believing in its existence, as well as your destiny in connection with it; and we have thus a kind of evidence that this interest does not exist on *your* side *alone*, but that it is felt as a reciprocation: it is shared, and, I believe, in an intenser degree, by the inmates of your Father's home.

It may be that this interest is somewhat deadened because you do not possess a physical vision of these translated beings and their doings. The Lord holdeth back from your view the face of his throne, and spreadeth his cloud above upon it; and he hides from you also the whole inmates of heaven, and he refuses to show to you what they are doing, and how they are acting, and how they are spending their glorious eternity.

But, though you do not *see* heaven and its glorious inhabitants, it does not follow that they do not see the earth, and you who are upon it; and you are not to measure their interest in *you* by your interest in *them*.

The inhabitants of Britain feel an interest in what is taking place in the various colonies connected with the empire: they feel this interest the more, that these provinces are under the sceptre of the same beloved sovereign. We know that this interest is reciprocal. The inhabitants throughout the different dependencies of our empire repay our solicitude; and they do more, inasmuch as we are objects of greater interest to them than they are to us. So we may infer, that a similar interest, for a similar reason, exists among the denizens of heaven, in what is taking place upon the old mother-country, earth. The same Sovereign rules over both worlds. Those who are the inhabitants of heaven feel an interest in the Sovereign who is in the midst of them upon the throne of his glory; and thus they will naturally feel an interest in all his subjects, and in the whole boundless realms over which in his high sovereignty he reigns.

CHAPTER II.

PHILOSOPHICAL EVIDENCES (*continued*).

2. *Heaven is a Home.*

 HOME, if it be a Bethel, the house of God, the habitation of a pious, loving, Christian family, is the fountain and centre of *interest* towards all who are connected with it. Children may be far distant in a foreign land; but the warm interest of home goes out after them and towards them, and reaches them through letters and presents, and kind inquiries, and holy and fervent prayers.

If heaven, then, be a home, it is surely legitimate reasoning to infer that the interest of those who are in it will be real and deep and fervent towards their younger brothers and sisters who are still dwelling upon earth, and who are preparing to join them in their celestial mansion.

3. *The inhabitants of heaven and God's children upon the earth constitute but one family.*

"For this cause I bow my knees unto the Father of our Lord Jesus Christ; of whom the whole *family* in *heaven* and *earth* is named." "For it pleased the Father that in him should all fulness dwell." "And having made peace through the blood of his cross, by him to reconcile all things unto himself; by him, I say, whether they be things in earth or things in heaven."

The Holy Spirit is in the bosom of one and all God's children, both in heaven and upon earth, as the Spirit of adoption, — their life, their love, their centre, their union. God is their Father; Jesus is their elder Brother, the connecting link, making the children of God *one*, both those who are in heaven and those also who are still upon earth. You who are believers feel an interest in *many* of God's children who are now in glory, if not in them *all*. You feel an interest in your now *glorified mother*, who has entered heaven before you; in your *father*, who has returned and come unto Mount Zion with songs and everlasting joy; in your beloved *child*, who came forth like a beauteous flower, which withered in the early spring of life, and which the Lord Jesus so early transplanted to the heavenly paradise, to blossom there in immortal youth. Do these *former* dear friends of yours, then, who are now in heaven, not *reciprocate* this interest? If you say that they do *not*, *where* is this set forth, I ask? and *what* is it that prevents them from cherishing this?

It is quite natural for the members of a family to feel for each other: indeed, it would be *unnatural* were they not to do so. The great mistake which many individuals commit, when thinking of this subject, is this, — they do not view God's translated children as a *portion merely* of his family, the *other portion* still dwelling in the nations and in the homes of earth. Avoid this mistake. Do not separate what God, by his Spirit, joins together and makes one. The whole children of God, both in heaven and upon earth, are *one* in Christ Jesus. Those who are up with God, if they possess the affection of children, and feel their relationship, through Jesus, to their younger brothers and sisters who are still in a state of grace below, *must* feel a loving care for them. Do not imagine that those who are in heaven are incapable of thinking, or that they never think about the earth.

4. *Those who are in heaven have a largeness of understanding and an extent of knowledge far superior to the children of God who are still dwelling upon earth.*

I infer, and, I think, legitimately, that their *increased knowledge* will dispose them to feel an *increased interest* towards all the members of the great family of God. Take, in illustration, the case of an ignorant, illiterate individual, who is totally unacquainted with geography, and who can neither read the Bible, to learn what is going on in heaven above him, nor even the newspapers, to learn what is transacting in the earth around him. You will find that individual exceedingly contracted in his views, as regards the subjects of his conversation, and the extent of his solicitude. Indeed, he feels no interest at all, and this just because his knowledge does not reach so far, in what so variously agitates the wide, wide world, in foreign courts and nations, or even in our own sovereign's palace, in the imperial parliament of Britain, and throughout our various colonies. Indeed, the world is almost a blank to such a person, and its doings make no impression upon him. *His* interest is centred in his own little locality, in the gossip of the village in which he lives, in the last tale of scandal that has been set in circulation by some busybody through the parish. What the world is to that ignorant and narrow-minded man, so is heaven to the mere groundling; yea, even to many a contracted and earthly-minded Christian.

Wherever, accordingly, we find in an individual enlarged knowledge and increased intelligence, there we also find an increased interest in the world's doings. His views are not circumscribed by the boundaries of his own little locality, and his interest is not absorbed in its transactions. What the learned are to the unlearned, the wide-minded to the narrow, so are the now glorified to the yet untranslated.

5. *Those who are in heaven are in possession of sympathy, and are thus capable of feeling an interest in the whole family of God.*

The philosophy of sympathy is the philosophy of the affections. It is that extraordinary process, which, found in the animalculæ and the man, forms *the principle* of association in the species. So general is it, and apparently so necessary, that we cannot even suppose how organized and sensitive beings could exist without it. But it is in its influence over masses, and in its aspect of a great overruling emotion, that it becomes of most interest to us. History affords us striking examples of such great movings in entire nations, and our own times are not without signal cases.

During the Russian war, a thrill of this universal power went to the very heart of Britain, when the intelligence reached our shores from the Crimea, and was circulated through the medium of the British press from town to town, and from home to home, that our brave soldiers there were perishing piecemeal, not by the bullets or bayonets of the enemy, so much as by a want of food and shelter, and by the murderous work in the trenches. During the Indian revolt and insurrection, the feeling was one of indignancy at the treason and cruelty of the Sepoys, occupying all hearts, and pervading the entire nation. We may thus learn something of the working of that power among the inhabitants of heaven. We are to look not only for the individual sympathies, but also those which, being true to the occasion, are general throughout one great division of mankind; even that already translated, and directed to the other, which comprehends the children of the world. The very name of sympathy implies reciprocation; and we have only to view it in the increased individual intensity pertaining to the wish that our friends should be saved from endless misery, to comprehend the intensity of the feeling spread, and increasing as it goes, through such myriads in heaven.

6. *The whole of the saved who are now in heaven were once the inhabitants of this very earth upon which we now dwell.*

It is from this earth they have entered the kingdom above. They are now there; but they were once here. Yes, *here* they were born; *here* they lived the shorter or the longer periods which the God of providence and salvation appointed them to spend upon earth; *here*, too, they were born again, through the quickening operations of the Holy Spirit, and became the new creation of God in Christ Jesus; *here* they spent their day of grace, whilst the Sun of righteousness was shining upon them from God's sometimes bright, and at other times cloudy, firmament; *here* they passed their lives in social intercourse with those who were near and who were dear to their hearts; *here*, in the midst of their sympathizing and often weeping friends, many of them fell asleep in Jesus, and their immortal and redeemed spirits rose, and went up, and entered into heaven, where they now dwell, and are as happy as even God can make them. And can we deem it *possible*, that those members of the human family (and there are multitudes in this position, whom no man can number), who have left God's green earth and gone up into his home, feel *no interest* in those they have left behind them, whose salvation they felt so much interest in when here?

CHAPTER III.

SCRIPTURAL EVIDENCE OF THIS INTEREST.

THERE are certain *doctrines* revealed, and there are also certain *events* referred to, in Holy Scripture, which plainly show, that those who are in heaven *do* feel an interest in us who are dwelling upon the earth.

DOCTRINES.

1. *The doctrine of our redemption.*

Redemption is a monument reared for eternity to prove the interest which Father, Son, and Holy Spirit have in us. Upon that monument is seen the inscription, "Herein is love; not that we loved God, but that he loved us, and sent his Son to be the propitiation for our sins." The creation of the world; of the successive generations of the human family; the preservation of that great work; the ever-watchful and providential care which he is exercising over it, whilst opening the hand of an unwearied and of an inexhaustible beneficence, and showering down upon us, his sinful and ungrateful children, innumerable gifts, both temporal and spiritual, — all show the interest which the adorable Godhead has in us.

God has never left himself without a witness of this; giving us fruitful seasons, as well as seasons of refreshing from the presence of the Lord, and from the glory of his power; filling our hearts with food and gladness, and feeding us with the manna from heaven. He is making the outgoings of the morning and of the evening to rejoice over us. Day unto day is uttering his speech, and night unto night is teaching us the knowledge of his love.

But it is the work of redemption which most conspicuously and strikingly manifests the *interest* of the Godhead in his children. "In this was manifested the love of God toward us, because that God sent his only-begotten Son into the world, that we might live through him." "Behold what manner of love the Father hath bestowed upon us, that we should be called the sons of God!" "For God so loved the world, that he gave his only-begotten Son, that whosoever believeth in him should not perish, but have everlasting life."

Try to realize, for a moment, that unsearchable love. When He, the Father, not only covenanted with Jesus, the Son of his love, for our salvation, but when he actually *bestowed* upon the world that wonderful gift, did the Father love Jesus *little*, and was he thus influenced to give up his only-begotten and well-beloved Son? No; but he loved the world and its sinful inhabitants *much*. And thus, "when the fulness of the time was come, God sent forth his Son, made of a woman, made under the law, to redeem them that were under the law, that we might receive the adoption of sons."

It now appears that the fulness of the time is come. The prophecies that for ages had foretold a promised Deliverer are now about to receive their fulfilment. Those who are waiting for the consolation of Israel are engaged in prayer day and night, that God would remember his covenant, fulfil his promise, and visit and redeem his people.

And not only the Lord's children here, but angels who are the undying courtiers in the palace of eternity, and the whole of the redeemed who are standing in their white robes before the throne, are upon the tip-toe of a deeply engrossing expectation which has so long been cherished in the high courts.

If we ask why Jesus thus comes to earth upon the mission of our salvation, the answer can be nothing else than that it is because of the *interest* which both the eternal Father and the eternal Son feel in our ultimate destiny. We are fallen and perishing and lost, and God pities us, and does not wish us to perish. Nor has he any other way to save us, consistently with the principles of his moral government over the universe and with the claims of eternal justice, but this, — the incarnation and humiliation and death of his only-begotten and well-beloved Son: yea, so great is his love, so great his desire that we should be saved, that he does not withhold, but freely gives up for us, the Son of his love, to suffer and to die, to deliver our souls from death, our eyes from tears, and our feet from falling; to compass us about with songs of deliverance; to put a new song into our mouth, even salvation.

2. *Christ's mediatorial reign upon the throne of heaven shows us the interest that exists in heaven towards us who are upon the earth.*

Though Jesus is upon the throne, he reigns not for himself only, but for *our* salvation. The kingdom, the power, and the glory, all belong to him. He is the King of Zion, he is the Lord of glory; yet all is subservient to this great end. "The Lord said unto my Lord, Sit thou at my right hand, until I make thine enemies thy footstool. The Lord shall send the rod of thy strength out of Zion: rule thou in the midst of thine enemies. Thy people shall be willing in the day of thy power, in the beauties of holiness from the womb of the morning: thou hast the dew of thy youth."

3. *In Christ's intercession before the mercy-seat of heaven, we see the evidence that there is an interest existing in the heavens towards us.*

Whilst the Holy Spirit is our Intercessor in the

court of conscience, the Lord Jesus is our Intercessor in the court of heaven. "We have an Advocate with the Father, — Jesus Christ, the righteous." "For Christ is not entered into the holy places made with hands, —which are the figures of the true, — but into heaven itself, now to appear in the presence of God for us." "Who shall lay any thing to the charge of God's elect? It is God that justifieth. Who is he that condemneth? It is Christ that died; yea, rather that is risen again; who is even at the right hand of God; who also maketh intercession for us." Christ's intercession in heaven is thus graphically referred to by the Apostle John in the Apocalypse: "And another angel came and stood at the altar, having a golden censer; and there was given unto him much incense, that he should offer it with the prayers of all saints upon the golden altar which was before the throne. And the smoke of the incense, which came with the prayers of the saints, ascended up before God out of the angel's hand."

An advocate has an interest in his clients whose cause he pleads. The *fact* that the Lord Jesus, in the economy of redemption, is our Intercessor with the Father in the court of heaven, shows the *interest* which he feels in us, as he bears us upon his heart, and pleads our cause, and procures for us the Holy Spirit, along with all those heavenly blessings which he died to purchase, and which he now lives and reigns freely to bestow.

4. *The Holy Spirit's procession from the Father and the Son, upon the mission of our personal salvation, shows the interest in us that exists in heaven.*

The interest which the Holy Spirit has in us, manifested in his mission of love to save us, is sadly, and to a most melancholy extent, overlooked by many Christians, as well in their conversational intercourse with each other, as in their prayers, in their preaching, in their writings, and in their actings of faith.

We are impressed with wonder and amazement when we think of this marvellous work, undertaken gratuitously by the mighty Maker of heaven and of earth; passing by the angels who fell; withdrawing the eye of his pity from them in their ruin; looking down from his throne in his sympathy and in his love upon us; and sending forth his only-begotten and well-beloved Son, upon a mission of humiliation and tears, to redeem us by bearing our sins in his own body, even to death.

But how little do we feel impressed with right, realized, and living gospel views of this most wonderful condescension! How much do we make of man's gratitude to man! The virtue is praised as containing in itself all virtues; and he who is without it is said to be the very worst of mankind, of whom almost any evil may be expected. How seldom are these views applied to the relationship between the creature and the Creator; between him who gets all, even that gratitude itself, so much more pleasant to the giver than to the recipient, and him who gives all, even life itself, yea, salvation itself, but for which life would be a curse!

With what feelings would you be penetrated, were you at this moment to look up from the page you are reading, and see the morning of eternity bursting forth upon you in its sublimity; and, as you held in your breath whilst you were listening, to hear the voice of the archangel proclaiming to a startled world, "*There shall be time no longer!*" and, moreover, to see Jesus, the second Person of the adorable Trinity, coming forth to the judgment; to hear the minstrelsy around him of attending angels and glorified saints; while around you there were springing from their graves in the churchyards a mighty throng to meet the train from above! And yet how strange and awful the thought, that all this may take place any instant! Nay, the time has already drawn so near, that the chance of its suddenly startling the world, even in our day, is so great, that, were an equal chance to involve the peril of some worldly possession upon which your heart is set, you would be filled with horror and dismay. But the difference is not difficult to account for. The prophecy has sounded; but man is asleep, and not only asleep, he is dreaming of gold, and the conventional distinctions of a sybaritic age. "What! know ye not that your body is the temple of the Holy Ghost, which is in you, which ye have of God, and ye are not your own?"

5. *The existence of the means of grace, in the visible Church of Christ, shows the interest which Father, Son, and Holy Spirit have in us.*

The means of grace are not the institutions of man: they are the ordinances of the living God; they are the divine institutions of Jesus, who is the Head of the Church; and we should never forget the great truth, that he has instituted them in love to the world, for the conversion of the unconverted, and for the edification of the children of God.

By neglecting the means of grace, you despise and neglect Him who ordained them. These institutions of grace ought to be your greatest delight. When the Christian sabbath shines upon you who are the members of Christ's Church, you may see the interest which the Lord of the sabbath has in you. When the church-bells ring throughout Scotland on the sabbath morning, to invite you, its Christian population, to leave your homes, and go up to your several churches, that you may join there in the public worship of the God of your salvation, you hear the interest which the Lord Jesus has in you: "I was in the Spirit on the Lord's Day, and heard behind me a great voice, as of a trumpet, saying, I am Alpha and Omega, the first and the last. And I turned to see the voice that spake with me; and, being turned, I saw seven golden candlesticks; and, in the midst of the seven candlesticks, one like unto the Son of man, clothed with a garment down to the foot, and girt about the paps with a golden girdle. His head and his hairs were white like wool, as white as snow; and his eyes were as a flame of fire; and his feet like unto fine brass, as if they burned in a furnace; and his voice as the sound of many waters. And he had in his right hand seven stars, and out of his mouth went a sharp two-edged sword; and his countenance was as the sun shineth in his strength. And, when I saw him, I fell at his feet as dead. And he laid his right hand upon me, saying unto me, Fear not; I am the first and the last: I am he that liveth, and was dead; and, behold, I am alive for evermore, Amen; and have the keys of hell and of death." When you listen to the man of God, the ambassador of Christ, preaching to you the glorious gospel from the pulpit as ye sit in your pews, you see Christ's interest in you; for, in the voice of the herald of the cross, you hear the voice of Jesus addressing you, who is the minister of the sanctuary and of the true tabernacle, which the Lord pitched, and not man. When you are privileged to sit down in God's banqueting-house at the table of communion, you see Christ's interest in you; for he instituted the ordinance of the Supper, and his covenant presence is in the midst of you, his assembled people, at its every celebration. The Lord Jesus meets you there, overshadows you with the cloud of his covenanting love; and partaking spiritually of his body, which is meat indeed, and of his blood, which is drink indeed, you are able individually, with the mystic spouse, exultingly to exclaim, "I sat down under his shadow with great delight, and his fruit was sweet to my taste. He brought me into the banqueting-house, *and his banner over me* was love."

CHAPTER IV.

SCRIPTURAL EVIDENCE OF THIS INTEREST (*continued*).

DOCTRINES (*continued*).

*HE mission of angels to earth shows us the interest which those who are in heaven feel in us.*

Heaven is the home in which angels permanently reside. "Their angels do always behold the face of my Father which is in heaven." "The chariots of God are twenty thousand, even thousands of angels: the Lord is among them, as in Sinai, *in the holy place*." "I beheld, and I heard the voice of many angels *round about the throne*, and the beasts, and the elders; and the number of them was ten thousand times ten thousand, and thousands of thousands." "And all the angels *stood round about the throne*, and about the elders and the four beasts, and fell before the throne on their faces, and worshipped God."

The word "angels" means "messengers;" and the high intelligences thus designated receive their names, not because they make their way through the heavens to execute God's command, but *because* they visit the earth to perform, in behalf of its inhabitants, his messages and will. Angels come down out of heaven, and meet at this lower creation's natal hour, like a number of rejoicing friends assembling in a home where a child has been born, and sing together creation's birth-song; even as this earth arose at God's command in its beauty and sinlessness, and took its place in the circle as one of the orbs in the system of the sun. An angel from heaven intimates, to the shepherds of Bethlehem, Christ's advent to the world. An angel intimates to Joseph, in a dream, Herod's murderous instructions respecting the young child. In the garden of Gethsemane, whilst the Lord Jesus is stretched in his agony with his face upon the ground, an angel from heaven strengthens him. An angel rolls away the stone from the door of the sepulchre where Jesus is lying and sleeping coldly and silently among the dead. Two angels appear to the bereaved and sorrowing disciples, in white apparel, upon the Mount of Olivet, at the very moment that Christ's ascension is taking place, and just at the time that he is disappearing from their view behind the veil of the intervening cloud, and thus addresses them: "Ye men of Galilee, why stand ye gazing up into heaven? This same Jesus, which is taken up from you into heaven, shall so come in like manner as ye have seen him go into heaven." On the great day of judgment, angels are "to gather the elect together from one end of heaven even to the other."

I believe that what Jacob sees at Bethel is still taking place in a mystical way. The ladder of Christ's mediation rests upon the earth; the top of it is reaching to the heavens; and, without intermission, the angels of God are ascending and descending upon it in their missions of watchfulness and love in our behalf. "Are they not all ministering spirits, sent forth to minister for them who shall be heirs of salvation?" "Because thou hast made the Lord, which is my refuge, even the Most High, thy habitation, there shall no evil befall thee, neither shall any plague come nigh thy dwelling. For he shall give his angels charge over thee, to keep thee in all thy ways. They shall bear thee up in their hands, lest thou dash thy foot against a stone." And all this shows us *their* interest in the earth.

The Bible gives us a description of God's dealings with this world during the long period of nearly four thousand years; and, during the whole of that long history, we are, by many incidental expressions, reminded of the *intense solicitude* which angels feel in what is going on, not in heaven merely, but on the earth also. These missions of angels are not to be looked upon by us as banishments from heaven, enforced upon them by Him who is Lord both of angels and of men. They are, on the contrary, willing embassages of joy.

Since the canon of Scripture was closed, and since the period when these inspired descriptions have ceased to be given of God's dealings with the human family, have angels ceased to take any interest in the affairs of earth? Because their missions of love to the world and in behalf of man are no longer recorded by the pen of inspiration, are they no more taking place? and are these angels not coming forth to visit us now? Have they retired up into their holy places to take their ease, and fold their hands in idleness, and to sit motionless in their seats of honor, yea, ever since the beloved disciple wrote these words?—"I Jesus have sent mine angel to testify unto you these things in the churches. I am the root and the offspring of David, and the bright and morning star." Have they, in short, like Jesus, one and all now ascended up, not again to visit earth until the last day dawns? In other words, have they ceased to feel any interest in what is going on among the children of the valley? It cannot be! *These* missions and *that* interest will only terminate, when, at the last day, the earth itself shall be burned up.

Angels are not omniscient, like Him who is seated upon the throne, the Lord both of angels and of men; but I have already alluded to certain circumstances which distinctly and plainly intimate that their knowledge is very great. It is as the ocean, whilst ours is as the small and circumscribed lake. It is as the sun, that has already been shining six thousand years;

whilst ours is as the candle that burns for a while and goes out. The youngest angel in heaven must be, at the least, nearly six thousand years old, whilst man upon the earth is but the creature of a day. Angels can fly and expatiate through the whole glorious realms of heaven, nay, the whole boundless universe, as well as up and down among the nations and the homes of earth; whilst we are circumscribed by miles.

Angels see the heavens spread around them in all their glory and magnificence. They know about, and they probably see from afar, the regions of that terrible hell into whose fiery bosom a portion of their number has fallen, the smoke of whose torment ascendeth upwards full in their view for ever and ever. They see the earth spread out like a visible panorama beneath them, as they look down upon it out of the windows of heaven, or as they fly over it, even as the eagle flies, and turns its sun-lit eye upon the plains. They see its inhabitants, and know that through Jesus they constitute a portion of the family of God. They know the value of the soul of man, which they beheld at first formed after the image of God, and which is capable of being transformed, through grace, into the holy image of the glorified Redeemer. They know the preciousness of Christ's blood, and the blessed fruits that result from a participation in his great salvation. They feel that Christ is their Covenant-head for eternity, as well as the Head of the Church; for God hath gathered together all things in him, both which are in heaven and which are upon the earth, — even in him. They thus feel that they belong to the same family in which believers are numbered.

7. *The glorified members of the human family who are in heaven feel an interest in us who are upon the earth.*

Even were there not a word in the Bible referring to the interest which God's children in heaven feel in the earth, I would be inclined to infer it from the *fact*, that angels who are now *their companions*, and who live with them in the same home of love, feel this interest. What is the subject of interest to one portion of a united and loving family is generally the subject of interest to them all.

Does the sailor who is shipwrecked, but who is picked up by the life-boat and is borne safely to land, feel less interest in the deliverance of his comrades who are still floating in the boiling sea, and struggling with its tumbling billows, than those landsmen do who crowd the shore in their sympathy, and exert themselves for their rescue, but who were never encircled by similar dangers? And do angels, who were never shipwrecked by sin upon the great ocean of existence, and who stand in no need of the life-boat of salvation, feel *greater* interest in the lost children of men, in their everlasting rescue from the great ocean of God's wrath, than those glorified ones of the human family do, as they stand in their robes of glory upon the shores of Immanuel's land, and are beholding the tumbling billows still around their former comrades with whom they once sailed the sea of life? I feel assured they do not.

Moreover, do not the glorified who are up in heaven now completely, and in every feature of their moral image, resemble Jesus? and are they not followers, imitators, of God? Then we know that Father, Son, Holy Ghost, feel an interest in the earth, in the spread of the gospel through the world, and in the salvation of the poor, perishing children of men who are exposed to danger through sin. As God is love, so are those also who are now glorified.

Paul thus expresses the emotions and desires of his soul towards Israel whilst in the world: "Brethren, my heart's desire and prayer to God for Israel is, that they might be saved." Has Paul no interest in the salvation of Israel now? If he has not, he is much changed in his present state of glory up yonder from what he was whilst in a state of grace upon earth. Isaiah thus gives expression to the wish of his heart, whilst down among us in this world, that the salvation of Israel were come out of Zion, and that the lamp of the glorious gospel were lifted up upon all the dark places of the earth: "For Zion's sake will I not hold my peace, and for Jerusalem's sake I will not rest, until the righteousness thereof go forth as brightness, and the salvation thereof as a lamp that burneth." Has Isaiah no interest in the spread of the gospel now? The apostles, at the command of Jesus, and immediately after his glorious ascension into heaven to sit down at the right hand of the throne, went forth in the name and as the ambassadors of their ascended Lord, to carry the message of salvation to the ends of the earth. God knows what they encountered of opposition and persecution and privation and danger, and even death itself; and have these apostles no interest in the spread of that gospel now? Let this exhortation tell: "Rejoice over her," — the fall of the mystical Babylon, — "thou heaven, and ye holy apostles and prophets; for God hath avenged you on her:" an exhortation implying that the apostles and prophets who are in heaven feel an interest in the spread of Christ's kingdom of glory and grace, and in the downfall of Antichrist. If they had not, they would not be called upon to rejoice when great Babylon falls. If they have not, then they neither resemble Him who is upon the throne, nor the angels who stand together with them before it.

Look for a moment to the fulfilment of that prediction, over which these apostles and prophets are called upon to rejoice. Lo! spiritual and mystical Babylon has come up in remembrance before God. The man of sin is destroyed by the brightness of Christ's coming. Peter's chair, the incarnation of superstition and idolatry and of all unrighteousness, is overturned, and is lying broken in the deserted palace through which popes and cardinals and proud ecclesiastics once stalked in their lordliness and arrogance, and he, perhaps the last pope, is lying spiritually dead beside that broken font of the fallen chair! Yes, Popery has tottered, and, like a mighty city full of iniquity, has fallen with a loud crash. The city of all abominations is laid desolate at the feet of the Almighty. Over this consummation — may the Lord God in his holy sovereignty hasten the period of its arrival! — the proclamation I have already quoted comes out from the throne, addressed specially and particularly to the two classes to whom I have referred.

The Apostle John was once in the isle that is called Patmos, for the word and for the testimony of Jesus. His whole soul was on fire for the success of the Redeemer's cause, and for the spread of the gospel, even as if his lips had been touched by a live coal from off the altar of heaven. And has that fire been quenched, its light extinguished?

Look at the emotions of love to the human race that have throughout a past eternity existed in the very heart of our Father. Consider the desires and longings, and eternal glowings of solicitude, for the salvation of the world, that exist and circulate in the bosom of Jesus. Observe the manifestations which the Holy Spirit makes in behalf of our salvation, whilst making intercessions for us with aspirations that cannot be uttered. Look at the care which angels have ever shown for the salvation of the perishing, and for the spread of Christ's glorious gospel. Then look at the *fact*, that the glorified in heaven constitute a *portion* of *that family* of which Christ is the *Head*, the other portion being made up of angels; and you will feel, I am sure, naturally and irresistibly led to infer, along with me, that these glorified ones, who are standing in their robes of white before the throne of God, *must* feel an interest in the earth, and in us who are upon it.

The glorified who are in heaven felt an interest once in the spread of Christ's gospel upon earth. They are at home now, and are living in the presence of their Father, and are walking through heaven with Jesus, their elder Brother; but if they have no interest in the world, and in the children of God whom they have left behind them here, then they are unsocial and selfish and unbrotherly children, standing cold and unfeeling and heartless, so far as their brethren upon earth is concerned, rejoicing in their own gladness.

It may be that you have been parted by death from friends once dear to you; may *now* feel, in the midst of the business and pleasures and sins of the world, *no interest* whatever in those departed friends who have fallen asleep in Jesus, and who have gone up and entered into heaven; indeed, you may perhaps never *now* think about them at all: but rest assured, be verily persuaded of this, that they feel an interest in *you* still.

CHAPTER V.

EVENTS SHOWING HEAVEN'S INTEREST IN US.

THERE are many *such events* mentioned in Holy Scripture. I will refer, in illustration, only to a few.

1. *The overthrow of Paganism, and the establishment of Christianity, under the Emperor Constantine*, is an *event* that awakens the interest of those who are in heaven, and causes a deeper if not a new tide of congratulation and joy to flow over all its happy inhabitants.

Over this transaction the glorified are called upon to rejoice. "And there was war in heaven: Michael and his angels fought against the dragon; and the dragon fought, and his angels, and prevailed not; neither was their place found any more in heaven. And the great dragon was cast out, that old serpent, called the Devil and Satan, which deceiveth the whole world: he was cast out into the earth, and his angels were cast out with him. And I heard a loud voice saying in heaven, Now is come salvation and strength, and the kingdom of our God, and the power of his Christ; for the accuser of our brethren is cast down, which accused them before our God day and night. And they overcame him by the blood of the Lamb, and by the word of their testimony; and they loved not their lives unto the death. Therefore rejoice, ye heavens, and ye that dwell in them."

The following is the commentary given of this passage by Burkitt, one of the most judicious of divines: "After Michael and his angels', Christ and his followers', victory over the dragon and his angels, over Satan and his instruments, here follows a solemn thanksgiving for the Devil's downfall. The saints in heaven join with believers on earth in their song of confidence and triumph. When they speak of God, they say, *our* God; and, when they speak of the Church below, they say, *our* brethren. Behold a sweet communion between the Church militant and the Church triumphant! Indeed, they constitute and make up but one Church, one family, one household: the whole family in heaven and earth is but one."

All the emotions of our moral nature are infectious and communicative. Thus, whatever gives joy to the saints upon earth, we may naturally infer, vibrates upwards to the heavens, touches the bosoms of the saints in glory, and circulates through all the hosts who surround the throne of God.

2. *The fall of Babylon, the overthrow and downfall of Popery,* is an *event* that sends a thrilling emotion of the intensest interest upwards, and throws a gush of the most delightsome joyousness through the whole population of heaven. "And, after these things, I saw another angel come down from heaven, having great power; and the earth was lightened with his glory. And he cried mightily with a strong voice, saying, Babylon the great is fallen, is fallen. . . . Rejoice over her, thou heaven, and ye holy apostles and prophets; for God hath avenged you on her."

3. *The universal spread of the gospel throughout the world,* the rising of the Sun of righteousness upon all the dark and benighted regions of the earth, the knowledge of the Lord going forth as the waters cover the channel of the mighty deep, the ends of the earth beholding the salvation of the Lord, is an *event* that attracts the notice of the crowding hosts in heaven, and circulates a tide of holy rapture far and wide through all their exulting and rejoicing ranks. "And the seventh angel sounded; and there were great voices in heaven, saying, The kingdoms of this world are become the kingdoms of our Lord and of his Christ; and he shall reign for ever and ever. And the four and twenty elders, which sat before God on their seats, fell upon their faces, and worshipped God, saying, We give thee thanks, O Lord God Almighty, which art, and wast, and art to come,

because thou hast taken to thee thy great power, and hast reigned."

4. *Christ's transfiguration is an event which shows the interest those in heaven feel in the transactions of earth.* The following is the inspired description of this most instructive incident: "And it came to pass about an eight days after these sayings, he took Peter and John and James, and went up into a mountain to pray; and, as he prayed, the fashion of his countenance was altered, and his raiment was white and glistering. And, behold, there talked with him two men, which were Moses and Elias; who appeared in glory, and spake of his decease which he should accomplish at Jerusalem."

Contemplate for a little this meeting that takes place upon the mount of transfiguration. Jesus appears there in his glory. His face shines like the sun, and his raiment becomes white like the light. In this transfigured appearance, you see a glimpse of the glory which he had with the Father before the world was. You see also, by contrast, the depth of humiliation into which the Son of God stooped, when he took our nature into conjunction with his divine, and came down into this world to seek and to save the perishing children of men.

Were you to see the highest archangel in heaven suddenly divested of all his high attributes, his splendor, and beauty of form, in which he stands before the throne of God, and to become changed into a worm of the earth; were you to see the sun in the sky all of a sudden eclipsed, shorn of his light, and changed into a clod of the valley, you would not see such a transfiguration, such a change, as took place, when Jesus, who stood throughout a past eternity, in all the glory of his divine nature, behind the veil that hides heaven from us, made himself of no reputation, and took upon him the form of a servant, and was made in the likeness of men.

Jesus was rich in the possession of all the attributes of the Godhead, rich in the praises of heaven, rich in the fellowship and communion of the Father and of the Spirit, through the whole roll of the eternal ages that are past; but for our sakes he became poor, that we, through his poverty, might be made rich. When looking at Jesus shining in such glory as he exhibited upon the mount of transfiguration, we are apt to imagine that we see something about him *there* and *then* that is extraordinary; a glory that did not inherently and eternally and unchangeably belong to him. But when we remember, that, whilst Jesus is man, he is also God, that all the fulness of the Godhead dwells in him bodily, should we not rather be inclined to wonder why it was that he did not exhibit that appearance always, whilst associating here below with his disciples, and whilst walking to and fro among the towns and villages and homes of Judæa? Upon the mount of transfiguration he draws aside the veil; and *there*, for the *first* and *only* time during his bodily sojourn upon the earth, he shines forth in his unveiled glory and majesty. I do not attempt to describe the Redeemer's appearance at this moment of his transfiguration. Any attempt to do this would only tend to becloud that ineffable effulgence, and subject me to the rebuke, "Who is this that darkeneth counsel by words without knowledge?"

We must be content with the conviction, that His unveiled appearance *must* be glorious, who, on the morning of creation, said, "Let there be light, and there was light;" who covereth himself with light as with a garment; from whose presence, on the morning of creation, there shot a beam that lighted up the long-previously benighted creation, removed the preceding night of eternal darkness, gave to the sun his noonday splendor, and to the moon and stars their silvery twinkling. His unveiled appearance *must* be effulgent indeed, and terribly resplendent, in whose presence the very angels of heaven, through all their shining and praising ranks, bow down, veil their faces with their wings, and unceasingly cry, "Holy, holy, holy is the Lord of hosts: the whole earth is full of his glory." That unveiled splendor and manifested glory *must* indeed be effulgent and awfully dazzling, whose appearing in our sky on the great and terrible day of the Lord is to bring a bright and lovely morning to the long, deep, dark night of the grave, — a morning that is to flash in upon the slumbering, and, on the part of the living, often-neglected and forgotten, population of the grave.

Fifteen hundred years had rolled over this world, bringing in their train many changes, since Moses, at God's bidding, went up to Mount Nebo, and there, with no human friend near him to close his eyes, died before the Lord, left his body upon the mount, ascended from earth, and entered into heaven. A thousand years had passed away, since Elijah, without tasting of death, ascended from earth in his chariot of fire, with his bright convoy of attending angels; taking doubtless a fond, lingering, but not a last look of the mountains and valleys and churchyards of earth, where others lay buried, whilst he was exempted from going down there to lie among them, and went up and entered into heaven.

We cannot tell what was passing in heaven, the unseen world, the home of holy and unchanging love, when the command went forth from God who is upon the throne to these two, Moses and Elias, selected from all the mighty assemblages of glorified saints who were standing along with them before the throne of God, to leave for a little the minstrelsy of heaven. These two glorified saints did not assuredly volunteer themselves to undertake this mission to the mount of transfiguration, to pay a visit to earth, where they once dwelt, and acted a conspicuous part among their fellow-men.

Neither can we tell whether or not theirs was a

solitary, unparalleled, and unprecedented visit to this earth, upon the occasion of Christ's transfiguration; nor whether or not they, or many, or all the redeemed, who are assembled in heaven and who dwell in it, are permitted by God to leave heaven at stated times to visit the world, and to walk with Jesus invisibly, and discourse with him inaudibly to those around; nor whether or not other patriarchs and prophets were privileged by God to relinquish for a little the praises of eternity, that they might pay to Jesus similar visits whilst he remained upon earth. We do not know why more of the redeemed did not accompany, upon this occasion, these two bright emigrants from these far-off shores, to mingle again for a little among the clouds and obscurities of time, to see in Christ's appearance the great effulgence he was to exhibit to the whole population of the skies, when he ascended and entered again upon the glory which he had with the Father before this world was. We can see, however, a peculiar significance in the selection by God the Father, upon this particular occasion, of these two special envoys from his court in the heavens.

The law and the prophets were until John. Moses is chosen as the living type of the law, as the impersonification of the Mosaic economy, and as the representative of all who were then *in heaven*, saved *from* and *through* that economy. Elias was distinguished among the prophets of the Lord whilst he remained upon earth, not by his writings, for he has left none, but by his works, his zeal for the cause of the Lord, and by his fearless, yea, thundering denunciations against the works and the workers of iniquity; and he is selected upon this occasion to represent the *prophets collectively* who were in heaven, one of whom had thus described the coming and the appearing of Jesus: "Who is this that cometh from Edom, with dyed garments from Bozrah? this that is glorious in his apparel, travelling in the greatness of his strength? I that speak in righteousness, mighty to save. Wherefore art thou red in thine apparel, and thy garments like him that treadeth in the wine-fat? I have trodden the wine-press alone; and of the people there was none with me: for I will tread them in mine anger, and trample them in my fury; and their blood shall be sprinkled upon my garments, and I will stain all my raiment. For the day of vengeance is in mine heart, and the year of my redeemed is come."

These two resplendent messengers from on high are thus most discriminately and appropriately chosen as the representatives of *all* the *children* of God who were *then* saved; and, in the selection of these two representatives of the whole Church triumphant, we see the *interest* manifested, *evidenced*, *proved*, which all who were *then* in glory, and, let me add, of all who are *now* in heaven, feel in the earth, in the accomplishment of Christ's mediatorial work upon it, and specially in the great, momentous, and solemn *event* of Christ's death, which he was to accomplish at Jerusalem.

How many grave thoughts occur to us connected with this great event! What consultations the glorified may have *had* with one another and with angels *before* this *representative mission* to earth took place; how long, previously to its taking place, the knowledge of it was known and circulated in heaven,—we cannot tell. Elisha and the sons of the prophets are aware a considerable time before of Elijah's ascension; and the whole tribes of Israel are aware that Moses was to leave them, and go up to the Mount of Nebo, and die. The sons of the prophets looked on, and witnessed Elijah leave the earth and rise towards heaven in his chariot of flame. The whole assembled Israelites beheld Moses leaving them. So, for any thing we can tell, the same thing may have happened to these two glorified saints, when they left the population of heaven again to revisit the earth.

Alike unknown, though not uninteresting, is the answer to the questions, whether or not the whole of the assembled hosts *saw* Moses and Elias leave their resplendent ranks; whether or not they accompanied them to the outskirts of the world of bliss, and saw them issue forth through the opened gates of the new Jerusalem, descend and shoot away from heaven towards the earth, like two shining stars passing down from the high firmament, to take their place for a little in the lower earth, and to carry with them thither the form and appearance with which they shone in heaven; or whether or not the whole assemblies of the skies, whom Moses and Elias came to *represent* in the presence of Jesus, saw them reach the earth, light in their descent upon the mount of transfiguration, and stand there face to face with Jesus in his glory. It is *possible* they did; nay, more, it is highly probable, — it is almost morally certain.

Whilst Moses and Elias thus appear upon the mount of transfiguration to represent the Church above, and the interest which the glorified feel in the earth in the mission of Jesus and in the accomplishment of his work, and whilst the three chosen disciples are there with Jesus, as the *representatives* of the Church in *gospel times*, the Shechinah, the symbolic cloud of God's presence and beatitude, so well known in Israel, overshadows the mount, upon which the Church triumphant and the Church militant, in their representatives, meet as *one*, the Lord Jesus Christ himself being the glorious centre, with the day-dawn and splendor of heaven appearing as if the sun shone from behind, and bordered with light, as if fringed with the emanations of the day-spring from on high.

Again: notice the *conversation* which Moses and Elias held with Jesus upon the mount of transfiguration. They spoke of the *decease* which he was to accomplish at Jerusalem. This conversation most distinctly and convincingly shows us that the event of

Christ's approaching death upon Calvary was awakening a deep interest among all the inhabitants of heaven. Did Moses and Elias, and through them the whole celestial inhabitants, show such an interest on the mount of transfiguration in the *anticipation* of Christ's death? and had they *ceased* to feel that solicitude when it was actually accomplishing without the gates of Jerusalem; when Jesus was extended in excruciating agony upon the cross; when the sun was turned into darkness, as if he had swooned, and become black in the agonies of death, at the sight of Jesus, his Creator, writhing in the throes of a fearful dissolution; when the rocks were rending; when the earth was trembling and shaking and crashing to its centre; when an invisible hand was tearing the veil of the temple from the top to the bottom; when the women were in tears; and when the whole of the disciples, with the exception of the Apostle John, were looking on afar off in the deepest anxiety and consternation?

Whilst the whole of the lower creation, far and near, above and below, near the cross and far away from it, was thus convulsed, and manifesting an awful interest in the bloody tragedy, was God's higher creation unmoved? Were the inhabitants of heaven unfeeling, uninterested, and quite untouched by the tides of sympathetic sorrow that were flooding the world below? Were they going on with their song of praise in heaven, just as if nothing unusual had been transacting on earth? Did the glorified *then* resemble a little child coming singing with thoughtless joy into the room, and near the bed upon which his or her father is lying in the agonies of death? But if the *anticipation* of Christ's decease was a subject of *such* interest, yea, anxiety, to the saints in glory, as is evidenced by the conversation of Moses and Elias upon the mount of transfiguration, what must have been the feeling caused by the *accomplishment*, the *endurance*, the actual *suffering*, of that decease, to the inhabitants of heaven!

Look to yonder home. A child of many a hope and many a prayer is upon her dying bed. The cup of affliction is put by God, who rules in providence, into that sufferer's young hand, and death is in the cup! That is a beloved daughter. Yes, she is the beloved of the whole household, — the light of her parents' eyes, the joy of her brothers' and sisters' hearts. She grew up in her beauty in that home of love, and blossomed into womanhood: but, alas for our fading joys here! an untimely frost has descended upon her opening spring; and, lo! it has suddenly withered the rose that but lately spread itself out upon her healthful cheek; it has caused the lily upon her brow to fade; it has bedimmed the gleam of gladness that but lately beamed from her eye; and she is lying there now in the tremblings and tossings and distressing sinkings of dissolution.

Is there no interest existing in the bosoms of the

other members of that family, whilst the evening of life is closing in fast around that sickened but still beloved one of their number, and whilst in silence, and with the suppressed emotions of sympathy and fear heaving their bosoms, they look on, and witness the sufferings of the poor invalid, and listen to the heavy groanings that bear evidence that the last closing scene is already near? The mother is in tears at her beloved's bedside; she is bending with a heaving bosom over her; she is wiping the large drops of perspiration from her forehead; and is ever and anon wetting the parched lips with wine, and kissing the fevered brow; the father's bosom heaves with grief; and the brothers and sisters are feeling most acutely the pain of parting with one whom they all love so well.

Is *this interest* felt, and do these emotions exist, in the home upon earth, where a beloved member of the family is sick and about to die? What, then, was the feeling, oh! what was the soul-thrilling emotion, that was pervading and stirring the bosoms of all that were dwelling in yonder home of love, which has no small family in it, when Jesus, the beloved of all, was upon the cross, and was sinking in the closing agonies! Oh! what were the ineffable sympathies that flowed through the Father's bosom, when from his throne he looked down upon the world in sackcloth, beheld the Son of his love in the agonies of dissolution, and listened to him enveloped in the horrors of deep darkness, as, lifting his voice, he exclaimed, "My God, my God, why hast thou forsaken me?" What the thrillings and dismay of the Holy Spirit, when he beheld the darkness of a terrible night descending upon the bosom of Jesus, and pondered the awful spectacle, knowing that, by the covenanted arrangements of the Godhead in eternity, he was not, by his enlightening and comforting influences, instantly to remove that darkness, and to bring into its place the light of returning joy, and the smile of the Father's love! What the heart-throes of angels, as they hovered upon their wings of light and love, trembling with emotion above and around the cross, and looking down upon the awful spectacle they saw upon and around the hill of Calvary! And what the wonder and sympathy of the glorified, as they beheld the cross, and Jesus upon it, heard his dying cry, or listened to their Father's declaration, "The hour is come," the time arrived, amid the revolving cycles of predicted events, when Christ's decease is *actually accomplishing* at Jerusalem!

CHAPTER VI.

EVENTS SHOWING HEAVEN'S INTEREST IN US.

(*continued.*)

5. A *SINNER'S repentance is an event that awakens an interest in the bosoms of all who are in heaven.*

These are the words of Jesus in reference to this important *fact:* "Likewise I say unto you, There is joy in the presence of the angels of God over one sinner that repenteth." "I say unto you, That likewise joy shall be in heaven over one sinner that repenteth."

A sinner's repentance is an *event* which often awakens a lively emotion in the bosoms of all Christians. Paul's repentance, and establishment in the faith, was an event hailed as a triumph by all the followers of Jesus; and afterwards thousands of believers sung for joy, and lifted to the God of their salvation the voice of thanksgiving, for that Paul had been led, in a season of mercy, to feel the godly sorrow for sin that worketh repentance not to be repented of. The father of the prodigal son felt his bosom tumultuating with joy and tenderness when he descried from afar the well-known figure of his now penitent child on his way back to the home of his youth, with a crushed heart and a contrite spirit; for he exultingly exclaims, "It was meet that we should make merry and be glad: for this thy brother was dead, and is alive again; and was lost, and is found." The broken-hearted mother, and poor, hungry, neglected, and cheerless children, — previously desolate souls, — feel an indescribable joy when they see their formerly drunken husband and father reclaimed through religion, and become a sober and an industrious man. The Christian mother and father rejoice over their careless and ungodly son, visited by the converting and saving grace of God, and turning his feet into the ways of His testimonies. The minister is all sympathy and gratitude when he contemplates the work of conversion and evangelical repentance manifesting itself visibly amongst his dear people; witnesses the glorious gospel of Christ, preached by him from the pulpit, carried home by the Holy Spirit to the hearts and consciences of his hearers; and beholds another and another among them not merely made to tremble as Felix did, but turned to the Lord, becoming partakers of the heavenly gift, tasting the good word of God, and feeling upon their souls the powers of the world to come. The Lord's people upon earth raise anthems of praise and thanksgiving when they see converts flying to Jesus as the doves to their windows; when they see troops of pilgrims pressing onwards towards the celestial city, and weeping prodigals on their way back to their Father's home, lifting, as they go, the humble eye of an appropriating faith to Jesus, the author and finisher of their faith.

Who has not felt his inmost soul glow with equal warmth whilst reading about the Pentecostal awakening that has come down upon the South-Sea Islands, or the accounts of the late revivals in America, in Ireland, and throughout many parishes of our own beloved Scotland?

But, in the passages of Scripture I have already quoted, Jesus himself announces, in the words of eternal truth, that this interest in a sinner's repentance is not *confined* to earth, — it embraces and fills a much wider sphere; that, in fact, *it vibrates upwards, and enters the crowded heavens;* runs as if with the inaudible throbbings of an electric conductor from breast to breast, and from rank to rank, throughout the world of glory. "There is joy in heaven over one sinner that repenteth."

That there *is* thus an interest felt among the inhabitants of heaven over a sinner's repentance upon earth, is not a mere *probability*, — a mere *supposition* made by man, in his fanciful musings and imaginative wonderings, respecting what *may* be existing in the world of glory in relation to man's salvation. It is expressly *asserted* by Jesus himself, who is the faithful and true witness; whose eyes are as a flame of fire; who looks abroad through all the boundless regions of creation, beholding with one comprehensive and omnipresent survey the whole inhabitants of heaven, of earth, and of hell. "Neither is there any creature that is not manifest in His sight; but all things are naked and opened unto the eyes of Him with whom we have to do."

The assertion which Jesus makes is, that, the moment in which the godly sorrow for sin is undulating and flowing through the bosom of the penitent sinner, there is a new joy circulating through the bosoms of all who are in heaven. At the very moment the publican is in the temple, not daring to lift his face to heaven, but is smiting upon his breast with downcast eyes, and is exclaiming, "God be merciful to me a sinner!" at the moment Paul is asking, struck down and stretched upon the ground, beneath the effulgent glory of Christ's unveiled presence, "Lord, what wilt thou have me to do?" at the very moment Mary Magdalene is standing behind her Lord, with her tears running down her cheeks in such a stream that therewith she actually washes her Redeemer's feet, and wipes them with the hairs of her head; at the moment Jesus, seated in glory at the Father's right hand, opens the windows of heaven, and pours forth the Pentecostal effusion of the Holy Spirit upon the multitudes who are assembled in the temple of Jerusalem, listening to the Apostle Peter preaching to them the gospel in the name of his exalted Redeemer, and whilst three thousand are crying in the agonies of conviction, "Men and brethren, what shall we do?" at the very moment the earthquake is shaking the prison, and a soul-quake is moving the bosom of the Philippian jailer, and he is putting the question to Paul and Silas, "What must I do to be saved?" at the very moment the poor, humbled, downcast sinner, *wherever* he is, and *however* circumstanced, is led by the gracious operations of the Holy Spirit to feel that he has a soul that needs to be saved, and who is crying to God for help,—*that individual* is the object of a deep and of an engrossing attention, and of a thrilling *interest*, to all the inhabitants of heaven.

The language which Jesus utters, when he tells us that there *is* an interest felt in heaven over the repentance of every sinner, at the very moment it is taking place upon earth, reminds us that there is a *communication*, such as we too seldom realize, betwixt the inhabitants of earth and those above. Such a declaration proves, that, however we may dream about the far-off kingdom, nevertheless the earth is such a near door-neighbor to heaven, that what is taking place upon its surface is not only *known*, but is *felt*, in the world of peace; showing that the *mode* of *communication* is quick and accurate betwixt the two worlds. Christ's language, in reference to a sinner's repentance, reminds us that the earth is not wandering along its orbit, in the face of these high heavens, unseen, unnoticed, and uncared for by the glorious and numberless inhabitants who are up in security, and in possession of the great reward. The language reminds us, that there is not such a distance, that there is not such a silent and sepulchral void stretching betwixt the two worlds, as many of us are apt, in our unrealizing and contracted views, to imagine; for, in the words I have already quoted, He who is upon the throne asserts, that the *sight*, or the *knowledge*, by *communication*, of the tears of a penitent within one of the homes of this world, sends up a new and exulting emotion among all the happy myriads who are congregated before the throne of God.

And let it not be objected, that the words which I have quoted are the only *two passages* in the Scriptures which expressly assert that there *is* joy awakened, and consequently an *interest* excited, among the inhabitants of heaven, over every returning wanderer upon earth; for even *one* distinct announcement made by God himself, in his truth-revealing and blessed Word, is enough to establish, to the satisfaction of every believer, any one doctrine or tenet. Besides, God did not give us the Bible to gratify a vain and never-satisfied curiosity about heaven, and about what is going on in it; but to instruct us in the mystery of salvation, and to point out to us the path that will, through Jesus, lead us to it.

The Bible is our spiritual chart upon the sea of life. The compass of the mariner gives him no description of the country towards which he is sailing,—it merely points silently in the direction in which the poles lie; and this enables him to sail on in the right course that leads to his wished-for haven. And when the Lord Jesus leaves for a season the bosom of the Father, the throne of glory, the praises of the skies, bows the heavens and comes down, lights upon the earth, and mingles among the children of this world, and speaks face to face with perishing men, it is but seldom, I admit, that he draws aside the veil of eternity, and speaks of what is going on *in* yonder home. Instead of doing this, he employs himself almost constantly in announcing to the lost what they must do to be saved. He ministers not habitually to the insatiable cravings of an idle and of a wondering curiosity, but he soothes and satisfies the emotions of the penitent's heart, by assuring him, through two distinct and emphatic announcements, that his condition at the moment of his repentance is the cause of a *new* joy, and awakens a *holy interest*, among all the inhabitants of heaven; and, consequently, he need not fear that he will be unpitied by God, and overlooked and neglected by the members of his great family.

This, my readers, was what the necessity of your condition required.

We find a parallel upon earth. Were any one of you called to take your stand upon the shore of the tempestuous ocean; were you to look forth, and survey the troubled bosom of the great deep upon which the storm-wind has descended, to heave its waters, and to roll them into great mountains, light of foot and giddy in head; were you to behold in the midst of the foaming waves a vessel that had become all unmanageable, driven and tossed (for the winds and the waves have gained the mastery over it), carried towards the roaring breakers, then dashed upon the projecting rocks, where it is in no long time shivered and broken in pieces; were you, in these circumstances, to venture your life for the deliverance of those who were drowning, to tie the rope round your waist, and swim out from the shore among the uproar of waters, to attempt the rescue of the shipwrecked mariner, as he lay near you floating, tossed up and down, and every moment about to sink into a watery grave,—you would not, I suspect, waste precious time in trying to raise your voice above the noise of the storm, with the object of describing to him the beauty of your country, the fertility of its soil, the number of its population, or even the *interest* which those crowding the shore feel in his deliverance. Your first and chief object would be to snatch the drowning man from a watery grave; to give him such directions as might enable him to reach the shore.

Sin is a storm-wind that has shivered every one of the noble vessels of humanity that has been launched successively from the dockyard of immortality by God himself. The great ocean of existence was once placid and calm, and the noble vessels God was preparing to send upon it were destined by him to sail over a tranquil sea, and to enter a peaceful haven of glory upon the shores of Immanuel's land. It is otherwise now. Sin has come down like a terrific whirlwind upon that once-calm sea. And now, in this very world, where all *might* have been peaceful and calm, the storm of God's wrath is upon every child of Adam; the rolling billows of divine displeasure are around us; the rugged rocks of perdition are towering and frowning upon us from the shore of the eternity that is before us; and the foaming breakers are roaring in our hearing, and they are, alas! not very far off. Oh! meanwhile we are about to sink.

But, lo, the Ark of Salvation is not far off! It is riding over the troubled waters, and is sailing tranquilly and peacefully in the midst of the spiritually shipwrecked and perishing and lost. Jesus speaks, in the hearing of those who are every moment about to go down, not so much of heaven, and of what is going on *in* it, as of the way in which the perishing may be saved and may *enter* it. Thus it happens, that Jesus, merely in an incidental manner, refers, in the two passages quoted, to the *interest* that is felt in heaven, and the *joy* that is awakened there, over the repentance of a sinner upon earth.

Your repentance, who close with God in covenant through faith in Christ Jesus, is the Holy Spirit's work; and, in the *greatness* of the *Agent* who performs it, you see the *importance* of the *work* that is *wrought* and *done*. Repentance is the Spirit's work; and this of itself shows that it is no trifle. Your repentance is your translation from death into life; it is your spiritual passage from a state of nature into a state of grace, from darkness into light, from the kingdom of Satan into the kingdom of God's dear Son.

In the momentous hour of your evangelical repentance, Satan loses a subject who was previously led captive by him at his will; God gains a once-lost child; Jesus receives a new subject into his kingdom of grace, and a new gem into his mediatorial crown; Satan's kingdom, to some extent, totters, and gives way; Christ's kingdom is advanced.

Your repentance, besides, is an event which you may reasonably believe is known in *hell*, as well as in heaven and upon earth. Fallen angels roam the earth, and strive to gain the mastery over your souls. "And you hath He quickened who were dead in trespasses and sins; wherein in time past ye walked according to the course of this world, according to the prince of the power of the air, the spirit that now worketh in the children of disobedience." "Put on the whole armor of God, that ye may be able to stand against the wiles of the Devil. For we wrestle not against flesh and blood, but against principalities, against powers, against the rulers of the darkness of this world, against spiritual wickedness in high places." When Satan and his fallen legions are dispossessed of the citadel of your soul, are driven from the garrison of your heart, are vanquished and overcome and thrown back by the mighty and divine influences of the Holy Spirit, the *tidings* of such an event, which these lost and now discomfited spirits will assuredly carry to the place of woe, will spread a deeper gloom and a fiercer glare over all the fiery caverns of the lost. The painful thrill of an ignominious defeat, such as is felt throughout a kingdom when a subject is lost, taken captive, and carried away, thrills through all the burning regions. Yes, those who are there feel in every such transaction that a soldier is lost to their army, and a subject is taken captive, and is carried out of their kingdom ; and this spreads over the whole of hell's vanquished and screaming population the distress and the horror of a sore discomfiture.

But, mourning penitent, the tidings of your repentance spread a very *different* feeling, and create a very *different interest*, among the inhabitants of heaven. Over your repentance, heaven rings jubilee ; and multitudes without number, feeling the thrill of a new sensation and the glow of a higher emotion of joy, pour forth their seraph-voices in this hallelujah acclaim : "Worthy is the Lamb that was slain, to receive power and riches and wisdom and strength and honor and glory and blessing." "*For* there is joy in heaven over one sinner that repenteth."

Penitents! returning wanderers! lift your eyes to the heavens. Think of the numbers there who are thus deeply interested in you. Look up with the eye of a realizing faith to your high home. Look in upon the living realities of the world of glory. Survey the numberless hosts who are before the throne of God, and who are even *now* rejoicing over your conversion, and over your entrance into the kingdom of grace. You may have many difficulties to encounter, and many cold repulses to meet, in making your peace with your fellow-men, whose character you may have vilified; whose good name, in the days of your thoughtlessness, sin, and malice, you may have tarnished; whose property you have filched, it may be, and embezzled, by your once impenitent hands. You may have much difficulty in restoring to those you have injured that which you robbed them of in the days of your sinning; but your repentance is not evangelical and true, without reparation made to those you have injured, and without a full and conscientious restitution made to those you have defrauded, of that which you have unrighteously taken from them. Zaccheus restores fourfold; Paul promised to repay to Philemon what Onesimus, who had nothing to give, had taken from him: and let these be your examples.

You may have the scowlings of the ungodly, and the well-founded suspicions of the children of God, to bear, in your return to a life of repentance and faith and new obedience: but take courage; persevere.

Advance unflinchingly in your present movement away from your sin, and in your entire and complete return into the covenant and into the bosom of your God. You are guilty: but look up; lift your eye to the throne of heaven. Lo! you see up yonder Jesus, the Lamb of God, reigning not merely in glory, but in love also, and in the sovereignty of his grace; and your comfort under a sense of guilt is, that his blood cleanseth from all sin. You are polluted; you feel that your sin has not only made you guilty, but that it has also made you impure, in the sight of a pure and holy God: but look up in prayer and in supplication; the Spirit of holiness is proceeding forth from the throne of God and of the Lamb, — the pure river of the water of life. He is the living water from the upper sanctuary, descending to wash you and cleanse you, and to give you a meetness to become partakers of the inheritance of the saints in light. You are homeless pilgrims. Here you have no continuing city and no abiding-place. You are but strangers upon earth, as all your fathers were; but look up. There is a home yonder, already prepared and furnished and made ready for you: it is the home of your Father; it is the home into which Jesus is about to receive you, that you may dwell in his presence for ever; it is the house not made with hands, eternal in the heavens. You feel, it may be, poor and neglected, and outcasts, compared with others who are pampered and rich, and upon whom, in their thoughtlessness and thanklessness, God is showering down the bounties of his providence: few, it may be, feel the slightest *interest* in you upon earth; but it is not so with those who are in heaven, if ye are now feeling that godly sorrow that worketh repentance not to be repented of. The day of grace is dawning upon your path. The shadows of a dark and dreary and a too-long spiritual night are for ever fleeing away. Over your spiritual birth, your repentance through faith in Jesus, your transition into a new life, there *is*, yes, there *is*, even *now*, a glow of new and intense interest circulating among all the inhabitants of heaven. God your Father, God your Saviour, God the Holy Spirit, is even *now* bending over you in love from the throne, feels the deepest interest in you, and readiness to clasp and infold you in the embrace of everlasting love. Angels are gladdened that you are now escaped from the wrath to come, and are delivered from the agonies of the second death, and from yon fearful hell into which you were about to plunge for ever. "Likewise I say unto you, There is joy in the presence of the angels of God over one sinner that repenteth." The glorified multitudes of the human family — those who have through much tribulation entered the kingdom of glory; indeed, all who are in heaven — feel deeply in your fate, and are rejoicing over your repentance, and return to God. "I say unto you, that likewise joy shall be in heaven over one sinner that repenteth."

CHAPTER VII.

EVENTS SHOWING HEAVEN'S INTEREST IN US,
(*continued.*)

MARK the *time* when the inmates of heaven feel such a deep solicitude in your welfare. It is not at the hour of your death, when the great spiritual conflict of a life of grace is over, and when you leave the battle-field of your present probation more than conquerors. It is not when you are falling asleep in Jesus, and when your redeemed and completely sanctified and already glorified soul is rising upwards to heaven, encircled by your escort of attending angels, and observed by those on high with earnest longings for you to come on, and with this question upon their joyous lips, "Who is this that cometh up from the wilderness leaning upon her Beloved?" It is not when you have just nearly finished your journey up into God's glorious heaven, and when you are in the act of entering into the gates of the city of the New Jerusalem, and when the bright assemblages who are before the throne have just got their attention first fixed upon you after your entrance, and as they look towards you drawing nigh to join their ranks. It is not when the Lord Jesus, who has upon his head many crowns, leads you up to the glowing, loving, unveiled presence of the God of your salvation, and crowns you with a diadem of glory never to fade, and when you are taking your place among the worshippers in heaven, and when you are just beginning to join for the first time in the anthem that rises and resounds through heaven.

On the contrary, it is when the *first arrow* of conviction reaches your heart. It is when the *first tear* of godly sorrow is trickling down your cheeks. It is when the *first penitential prayer* is yet upon your trembling lips; whilst you are, like the Psalmist, looking up to God, and are giving utterance to these words: "Out of the depths have I cried to thee, O Lord!" It is when you arise in the strength of the Lord God Almighty, and are taking the *first step* in your return to a state of grace, and to covenant peace with your Father in heaven. It is when the recording angel is yet in the act of writing down your name in the Lamb's book of life. *Then* it is that a new thrill of joy rolls through the heavens, and is felt and is shared by all who are dwelling in the world of glory.

Had it not been thus expressly and distinctly revealed in the Scriptures, we could never have known that any event occurring upon the surface of this earth was positively known in heaven, or could awaken solicitude there, or could spread abroad, far and wide among the hosts, a new feeling into their always happy and rejoicing spirits.

We believe, indeed, in the *existence* of a heaven of glory above us, with Jesus there enthroned in mercy; but we have in our thoughts *removed* heaven to a *mighty distance*. Why have we reasoned ourselves into this state and belief? The answer is simple. The realization of a holy heaven that is quite near to us would give us pain, just as the presence of a holy man is an annoyance to one who is ungodly and impure.

Yes, *we* live in this world thoughtless and careless about those who are in heaven; and we have succeeded, through the sad and unfortunate possession of an unbelieving and of an undevotional heart, in reasoning ourselves into the belief, that they feel just as little interest in us; upon the same principle, that, because we feel but little love in our hearts to God, we are apt, most improperly and illogically, to infer that God feels just as little love to us.

This assuredly is wrong. You see an illustration of the falsity of such reasoning, when you look at what is taking place among the members of a family upon earth: and be it remembered, that all God's children, both up and below, constitute but *one* family; they are all *one in Christ Jesus*. You have, perhaps, seen a young man leave his father's home in the country, and take up his residence in the crowded city, either in the prosecution of business or pleasure or learning. You have seen him, or heard of him, meeting there ungodly companions, and being seduced by them from the paths of virtue and of peace. You have at last seen him, who was once so attentive to his friends and so affectionate to his sisters and brothers, forgetting the father who once watched over him with affectionate care; the mother who nursed him and reared him so tenderly and kindly; the brothers and the sisters, who once, in all the joy of innocent mirth, gambolled with him through the rooms of the same happy and loving home. The prodigal son had to come to himself before he recalled to his recollection the home of his youth, and his neglected father who still lived in it, with all the glow of an unquenched affection in his bosom, and with many fond recollections in his memory clustering in their warmth and freshness around his absent child. But tell me, my readers, when the profligate young man *succeeds* in thus *banishing* from his thoughts the remembrance of his father and of his father's home, and the many kind and endearing memories connected with his mother and sisters and brothers, who are still dwelling there, with hearts glowing in the fire of the old affection, do his father and mother and sisters and brothers *also* succeed in *banishing* from their thoughts all remembrance of him? Assuredly no! The prodigal son had to *awaken* to a sudden recollection of his loved and loving home, from which he was distant far, in the land of the stranger, and in the hungry wretchedness of his misery, before he arose, and began his journey homewards. But had the father also forgotten him? No: the father seems to have been out, as he probably every day was, looking forth in the direction in which his still-remembered son had gone when he left, longing, with all the unutterable yearnings of a father's heart, for his long-lost but still fondly-loved one's return; when, lo! suddenly and unexpectedly he sees him from afar; and in a moment, as his son emerges into view, all the feelings and kind emotions and past remembrances of a father stream through his gladdened heart. "And he arose, and came to his father; but, when he was yet a great way off, his father saw him, and had compassion, and ran, and fell on his neck, and kissed him."

We were once, as a race, in the happy position of the prodigal son before he left his father's home. We dwelt in Eden, beneath the smile of our Father in heaven, and encircled with the sunshine of his favor and love. We lived in love with heaven then, and walked in the covenant of our God. The earth was glad around us, our heart was holy and happy within us, and the heavens above were smiling over us. The roses of Eden clustered around us, breathing forth their fragrancy wherever we walked in the gladness of our heart. All was then light and love, both in our soul and in the creation around us; except in the place of woe, where fallen angels were lying chained and burning.

But, in an evil hour, we hearkened to the voice of the tempter. We sinned. We went out from Eden, as the prodigal son from his home of love. We went out from the constant and holy realization of God, and from habitually holding our pristine high and joyous communion with him. Soon, as a race, we sunk into such a state of alienation from God, that these words of Scripture give us but too true a description of our position: "Without God, without Christ, and without hope in the world."

In our alienated condition, and whilst we remain in a state of nature, we live in the world here unmindful of God, and in a state of the most profound thoughtlessness and carelessness about those who are in our Father's home. But tell me, *has Father, Son, and Holy Ghost,—have the living and glorious and happy and loving inmates of heaven, also forgotten us?* Let the great work of our redemption tell. Let the love of the everlasting Father, thinking of us in the high councils of heaven, making his covenant arrangements for our deliverance, and freely giving up his Son for our salvation, tell. Let the coming of Jesus from heaven to earth, upon the great mission of our salvation, tell. Let the descent of the Holy Spirit from the Father and the Son into the ruined and dilapidated temple of our soul, to build it up again in the very image of God, and to make us the new creation of God in Christ Jesus, tell. Let the visits of angels to this world of ours, in every age of its history, tell; for they are all ministering spirits, sent forth to minister to them who shall be heirs of salvation. Let the visit of Moses and Elias from heaven, to meet with Jesus on the mount of transfiguration, and to talk to him there about his decease, tell. Let the deep thrill of interest and of holy joy that rises to heaven, and the kindling glow of a generous sympathy that spreads far and wide among its rejoicing inhabitants, over every sinner's repentance, tell.

These things plainly and distinctly bear evidence, there is a voice that comes out from them, and which audibly announces to us this great truth, — that although we, in the midst of our sin and alienation and spiritual darkness and earthly-mindedness, have *forgotten* God, and all the exalted and holy and happy inmates of a high and glorious eternity, yet they have *never*, no, *never*, for one moment, forgotten us; and so deeply interested are they in *us*, in our repentance, our conversion, our return to God, that the sound of our returning footsteps, and the heaving sigh of our broken heart, sends upwards a new thrill of joy into the bosoms of all who are in heaven.

We are not informed by Jesus of the *way* or *mode* in which those who are in heaven gain a knowledge of our repentance at the very moment in which it is taking place; nor would it be right in us dogmatically to assert the *precise mode.*

This may be done in *three different ways:* First, He who is upon the throne — Father, Son, and Holy Spirit — may announce our repentance the moment it occurs to those who are before the throne, in the same way that a sovereign, in his palace upon earth, makes known to his courtiers any important event that has taken place in his dominions, the tidings of which have just reached him; or in the same way in which a loving father, who is at the head of a family, communicates orally some remarkable occurrence to the children of his affection, and to the rest of the inmates who compose his domestic circle, — such a communication being the spontaneous act of his love. Second, The inmates of heaven, for any thing we can tell, may *see* us, as they look upon us out of heaven: thus the view of our appearance, the tears streaming from our eyes, and our countenances bedimmed with sorrow, may be the means of giving them the knowledge of our repentance; in the same way that our friends upon earth come to know our repentance by marking our throes and ejaculations, and entire change in our conduct of life. Third, Angels ascending from earth may announce our repentance to the inmates of heaven, when they rise from our homes, where we are prostrated before God in the tears and sorrow of evangelical repentance, and repair to heaven.

We have reason to believe, that what Jacob witnessed in his dream at Bethel is constantly taking place throughout the earth. The ladder of Christ's mediation rests upon the earth, whilst its top is reaching the skies; the angels of God are ascending and descending upon it, — the celestial aides-de-camp that are carrying on a constant communication betwixt Christ, the Captain of salvation, and believers, who are engaged in conflict with principalities and powers, and the ruler of the darkness, upon the battle-field of this lower earth.

In every case of repentance, Satan suffers a defeat, and Christ gains a victory. When the tide of battle thus runs in favor of the Cross, and when the standard of the gospel is unfurled, and is spread over the citadel of another conquered heart, angels rejoice, and watch the issue of the conflict that is going on betwixt the followers of the Lamb and the slaves of Satan; and it may be, whenever we are brought to feel before God that godly sorrow for sin that worketh repentance not to be repented of, one of these angelic messengers who has been watching over us feels a new emotion, yea, a sudden gush of uncontrollable joy, and, unable to restrain himself, spreads out at once the wings of an exultant jubilation, rises, leaves us in our tears, ascends upwards, and still upwards, till he reaches the world of glory, enters heaven, and at once announces our name, in the hearing of all who are there, as now a true penitent, — a child of God. It is this intelligence from earth that awakens a new joy in heaven because another child is born into God's great spiritual family; another wanderer is arrested in his path of alienation and sin, and his returning footsteps are already directed towards the opened door of his Father's home; another captive is snatched for eternity from the hand of the spoiler; another gem is placed by the hand of eternal love in Christ's mediatorial crown, to shine there for ever; another perishing immortal is saved. Yes, over this event a new tide of joy rolls with its crystal waters of exultation over the gladdened population of the skies; a new harp is struck; a new worshipper joins the praising myriads; a new chorus rises in the temple of glory; a louder anthem of praise ascends in its roll of symphony before the throne of God.

I now address myself to you who may read these views. I ask, Is Jesus upon the mediatorial throne, high and lifted up, having all power in heaven and upon earth? Is he sending the rod of his strength out of Zion? and has it struck the flinty rock of your heart, so that the waters of contrition are flowing forth? Is Jesus now riding forth in the chariot of the everlasting gospel, conquering and to conquer? Has he girded his sword upon his thigh in his glory and majesty? and have his arrows pierced your previously hard and stony heart, doing thereto what the rod of Moses did to the rock of Horeb, — turning the rock into a standing water, and the flint into a fountain of waters? Has the Holy Spirit descended from the eternal Father, and from the glorified Son of his love, upon the mission of your personal salvation, and, in his living and quickening operations of grace, entered into the chamber of your heart? Has he just commenced the work of conversion there, of regeneration, of the new birth, working within you the good pleasure of God's goodness, and the work of faith with power; the commencement of a great spiritual transition from a state of death into a state of life; the beginning of a passage out of a state of darkness into the marvellous light of the glorious gospel of the grace of God? Is the morning of a spiritual day just beginning to dawn upon your benighted soul? Is the day-star of eternal promise, with its orient twinkling, just emerging into view, and flinging its bright radiancy around you? Are you now, in short, before God, and beneath the glance of his pitying eye, a *sincere penitent?*

You may, in these circumstances, as I have said, be neglected and uncared for by the men of the world. The votaries of pleasure, in the midst of their music and dancing, may turn away from you, and may have no pitying look to bestow upon you. Your present state and spiritual transition, however, let me remind you, is not unnoticed, and is not unobserved. Nor is this joy over you confined to earth: soon it is to be known and proclaimed in the high court of the Lord.

The cry, "A reprieve!" sends a deep and throbbing sensation among the assembled crowds who surround, in breathless anxiety and perturbation, the scaffold, upon which is already standing the poor condemned criminal, pinioned, agitated, trembling, and pale, when, just at the right moment, that reprieve comes down from the throne, and is borne and is held up — that the executioner may stay — in the hand of yonder approaching furious rider, whose galloping steed, with its nostrils distended and its sides panting, is all white over with foam. The cry, "Victory!" lifted by the coursing aide-de-camp on the field of battle, raises a shout of joy from the hearts of the soldiers of the victorious army; and the sound follows that flying messenger as he gallops along the fatigued but brave and still undaunted ranks, making known to all the victory is won. The cry, "A penitent, a penitent!" announced by the ascending angel, who has just left you in your tears, entering, even now at this very moment, into heaven, agitates the whole inmates of glory, even as a breeze, suddenly springing up on a calm, peaceful summer afternoon, sweeps with its rushing surges over the forest, and moves the leaves wherever it passes, or descends upon the surface of the lake, and causes the eddying ripples to circulate over the bosom of its previously silent and sleeping waters; and, wherever that cry runs, the whole population on high is moved; the song that rises from heaven's congregated assemblies becomes louder in its swellings, as it rises in one loud, sweet roll of commingled melody before the throne of God, and thousands upon thousands pour forth their seraph-voices, loud as the noise of many waters, and deep as the rumbling roll of mighty thunderings, saying, "Alleluia, Alleluia! the Lord God omnipotent reigneth!" Let us be glad and rejoice, and give honor to Him; for the marriage of the Lamb is come, and another and another spiritual bride upon earth is making herself ready: "*for* there is joy in heaven *over one sinner that repenteth.*"

CHAPTER VIII.

EVENTS SHOWING HEAVEN'S INTEREST IN US, (*continued.*)

MARK the *universality* of this joy in heaven over your repentance. "What man of you, having an hundred sheep, if he lose one of them, doth not leave the ninety and nine in the wilderness, and go after that which is lost, until he find it? And, when he hath found it, he layeth it on his shoulders, rejoicing. And, when he cometh home, he calleth together his *friends* and *neighbors*, saying unto *them*, *Rejoice with me;* for I have found my sheep which was lost. I say unto you, that likewise joy shall be in heaven over one sinner that repenteth, more than over ninety and nine just persons, which need no repentance." All who are in the shepherd's house, together with the friends and the neighbors who assemble there, mutually share in the joy that is felt when the previously wandered sheep is brought back to the fold.

There is the same *universality* of joy among those who are in the woman's house, when, after a diligent search, she recovers her lost piece of money; and which is graphically illustrated in the following parable: "Either what woman, having ten pieces of silver, if she lose one piece, doth not light a candle, and sweep the house, and seek diligently till she find it? And, when she hath found it, she calleth her friends and neighbors together, saying, Rejoice with me; for I have found the piece which I had lost. Likewise I say unto you, there is joy in the presence of the angels of God over one sinner that repenteth."

The same *universality* of joy among all who are in the home is illustrated and taught us in the parable of the prodigal son; who, rising up from the lap of sinful indulgences in the land of the stranger, returns to his home, and is received by his father with kisses of joy. Nor does the father alone rejoice over his son's return. No: through these words of inspiration, look in, and see what is passing in that home over the return of that young man, who is shaking hands with all who are around, and who is now arrayed with the best robe, with a ring on his hand, and with shoes on his feet. "And the son said unto him, Father, I have sinned against Heaven, and in thy sight, and am no more worthy to be called thy son. But the father said to his servants, Bring forth the best robe, and put it on him; and put a ring on his hand, and shoes on his feet; and bring hither the fatted calf, and kill it, and let us eat, and be merry: for this my son was dead, and is alive again; he was lost, and is found. And they began to be merry."

If, then, heaven is a home, and there is now a great family in it, surely, upon all the principles of fair and analogical as well as logical reasoning, I am entitled to infer that the same sympathy, that the same communication and interchange of thoughts and feelings, that pass and repass and circulate among the members of an affectionate family upon earth, are existing and circulating and reciprocating among all the members of God's great family above. Angels constitute merely a part of that family: they are one, through Jesus, with the glorified who are there. All who are in heaven constitute but *one family*, *living* in *love* in the *same home:* thus whatever is the cause of awakening a new or a higher tide of joy in the bosoms of a *portion* of that family will be shared in and felt by all who are continually rejoicing in the presence of God above.

If this, then, be true, — and that it is, analogy asserts, and the Scriptures do not deny, but, on the contrary, most unequivocally and distinctly confirm, — if you are even now a convicted and converted penitent, and a humble suppliant at a throne of grace, the joy that is felt in heaven over your repentance is not confined to *one portion* merely of heaven's exulting inhabitants: it will run and stream from bosom to bosom, from rank to rank, and from one congregated mass to another, till it reaches the outskirts of Immanuel's land.

There are some, it may be, *now* in heaven, who were nearly and most affectionately related to you whilst they yet remained with you upon the earth; and in Christ Jesus, *your* and *their* new Covenant-Head, they are nearly related to you still. Let me give one example, for the sake of its universality and influence. Had you a dear, dear, fond mother once, who first learned your infant lips to pray to your Father who is in heaven? Did you often and often bow the knee, in the joyousness and gladsomeness of youth, beside her in prayer? and, in the lisping accents of childhood, did you ask from God the new heart which he alone can bestow? Can you look back through the bright vista of memory upon the time, as upon a vision of devotion commingled with love, when you saw her oft and oft upon her knees, in secret prayer, at the footstool of God's throne of grace? Did you hear her pray, not for herself alone, but for you, whose name she sent up in earnest supplication to her heavenly Father? Did she ask the God of salvation to bless you, her then hope and delight, whilst you wondered to whom your mother was addressing herself? for you saw no one in the room besides yourself, and she was not speaking *to* you, but *about* you. Did you grow up, and come to mature years, and live thoughtless about your mother's pious and heavenly instructions and holy example? Did your dear mother die whilst ye were yet in your alienation from God? Did you visit her upon her death-bed? Do you remember the impressive sight you witnessed, as you entered into her death-chamber, — her pale and haggard countenance; her sickly, failing eye, with which she looked out upon you from her dying pillow, as if from the very confines of the eternal world? You cannot but remember how thin and how pale her hand was with which she pressed yours, when she bade you a sorrowful adieu; nor how agonizingly anxious that look was with which she gazed into your face, and charged you, in the name of the great God, no longer to trifle with your soul and with the things that belong to your peace, but, as in the view, and already near the verge, of an approaching eternity, to wrestle with God day and night for the salvation of your soul, and to seek through the blood of Jesus for the pardon of your sins. Did you see your dear and beloved mother die, and go the way of all the earth? — attend, with others, her funeral? Did you encircle her newly opened grave? Did you let down the coffin, the lid of which hid from your view her changed countenance, into the cold and narrow bed of death; see the grave filled up; bow to the mourning and sympathizing attendants, who had met with you to perform the last sad office of friendship to the sleeping dead? You left your mother there in her sleep. Oh, deep is the sleep of the dead! Dreamless is their still and unbroken repose! Low is their bed of dust! Cold is their pillow! Did you, for a season, after her death and funeral, forget your mother's dying exhortation; the heaven into which she had ascended as her eternal home; the God whom she was praising, and in whose presence she was singing the song of salvation, and enjoying the beatific vision? — forget Jesus, whose face she was looking upon amid the light of a glorious eternity? and did you live in the world as if you were never to die?

Is it different with you now? Has God awakened you and brought you to yourself by the afflictive dispensations of his providence, by the preaching of his Word, or by the vision of your mother in the dreams of the night? Whilst in your dreams, did the vision of your mother, all love and all smiles, kneeling at a throne of grace as of yore, and praying for you, pass before your gazing and restless eye? Did that vision cause the young and comparatively holy and hallowed recollections of the past to rush in upon your soul with a startling gush of reproach and shame? Did God's Spirit descend upon you through that vision, and awaken you to the light and the gladness of a new spiritual day? Is the resurrection of your risen Redeemer the symbol of the spiritual rising from the dead which you are now undergoing through the quickening operations of the Holy Spirit upon your soul? Are you rising with Jesus to newness of life? Are you now, in one word, *a penitent?*

Certain thus as it is that your *now* departed mother felt a deep, an agonizing interest in your salvation, whilst she yet remained with you, let me now ask, Has she *ceased*, *now* that she is in your Father's home, to remember you, to long for your salvation, or to feel any interest in your spiritual welfare and in your eternal destiny? Oh, no! She has an interest in you still, and she has upon her redeemed soul a full remembrance of you as she stands before the throne of God; and assuredly Christ has an interest in your present repentance as well.

I might take another example also, for the sake of its universality, and power over the heart. Had you once a beloved father, who entered for you into covenant with Father, Son, and Holy Ghost, when you were given up to God in the ordinance of Christian baptism? Did he walk himself with Jesus in faith and in love, and in the covenant of his God? Do you remember the time when he first took you up, leading you by the hand to God's house of prayer; when you sat beside him in your family-pew, and looked with the commingled feelings of wonder and of awe to the man of God in the pulpit; and when you, for the first time, listened to the minister addressing you, and the congregation around you, about something which you felt was undoubtedly of great importance? for he looked so serious, and spoke so earnestly, and the people appeared so attentive; but you did not understand what he was speaking about.

Do you remember also the time when your father, as the high priest of your little family circle, morning and evening, led your devotions, and prayed with all the unction of a holy fervor for your salvation, and how humbly, how holily, and how devoutly he walked with God?

These holy scenes of your youth now appear to you like far-off visions of happiness, and of heavenly joys that are gilding the retrospected horizon of the past. Your father died whilst you were yet young. Did you grow up a giddy and thoughtless and ungodly young man? Were you to-day, the sabbath of the Lord, in God's house of prayer? Did you feel an unusual interest in the exercises of the sanctuary, whilst the man of God brought before you, and described so vividly and alarmingly, the case of your alienation from God, and God's desire, notwithstanding, that you should be saved?—God upon a throne of mercy, still waiting to be gracious; Jesus, a mighty Saviour, able and willing to save you; the Holy Spirit striving with your conscience to lead you to flee from the wrath to come, and to close with Jesus in covenant through faith; the day of grace fast passing away; eternity, an awful eternity, already near, lowering over you, and opening its bosom to your view, full of blackness and of tempest and of fire? No time to lose! Whilst Christ's ambassador was to-day proclaiming the gospel of his grace, did you feel that the Spirit of God was verily present with you, carrying home the word preached to your heart with demonstration of the Spirit and with power? Did you quake and bow before God, like the willow before the passing wind, and put the question, "What must I do to be saved?" In your chamber, all alone, after your return from church, the world shut out, and you shut in with God, do you feel an awfulness of solemnity, a deep and terrible silence, as if Nature were hushed by some great voice speaking out of eternity, and were in the act of listening? and are you led to listen, as if with suppressed breathing, for the occurrence of something that is to startle the nations, for the bursting-forth of Jesus from heaven into your view in all the glories of his fully manifested presence, for the resurrection of the dead, for the judgment of the world? Are you now constrained to pour out your earnest desires before God in prayer? Are you opening the door of your heart for the entrance of the Holy Spirit of God to create you anew, and to awaken within you that godly sorrow that worketh repentance not to be repented of? Is this your prayer?—"Come from the four winds, O breath! and breathe upon me." "Awake, O north wind! and come thou south; blow upon my garden, that the spices thereof may flow out. Let my beloved come into his garden, and eat his pleasant fruits."

Under the Spirit-breathing influences from a risen Saviour, are ye now born from above? Have ye become spiritually alive?—truly now, and sincerely, a penitent in the presence of God? Oh! there may be a tide at this moment of bitter and harrowing sorrow for sin circulating through *your bosom;* but *over* you, and *above* you, and *towards* YOU, there is *joy in heaven.*

Your guardian angel has witnessed the tear of your penitential sorrow; has had his attention arrested by the long, deep-drawn sigh which is heaved by the throbbing heart; has seen you upon your knees; and has witnessed the earnestness and the fervor of your supplications at a throne of grace.

What has this view of you led him to do? He has already ascended; he has risen up, from your side and from your room, with a holy alacrity, upon the wings of exultation and delight; he has even now, it may be, just entered his native skies, his bosom heaving and tremulous with the glad tidings which he bears up from your chamber, and which he is about to announce to all who are in heaven. Yes, up yonder, in the world of glory, in yon home where the bright and the blest are spending a happy eternity, and in which your already glorified *father* dwells, when the ascending angel enters and announces your name, and proclaims in the hearing of all heaven's listening hosts that you are *now a penitent*, he will exult.

And so we might extend those examples to cases not of such universal application, but with scarcely less influence. Have you a *sister* now in heaven, who once walked with you in the ways of God upon earth? or a *brother* now there, with whom you once took sweet counsel, and went up to the house of God in company? Have you a *son* now there, who remembered his Creator in the days of his youth, and who once longed, with all the unquenched and unextinguishable fervor of a young convert, that you should turn your face towards Zion, and begin without delay to accompany him in his journey to heaven, and advance side by side with him in the divine life? Or have you now a *daughter* up yonder, who once gave to you, and to those around you, a lovely specimen of sweet and heavenly piety whilst she yet remained with you? Have *these*, who once walked with you in the covenant of your God, and who dwelt with you once in the same home of love here, fallen asleep in Jesus? Have they left you in your bereavement? and has this world, by their departure, become to you a vale of tears? Are they now the inmates of heaven? and are they become, through grace, the happy members of your heavenly Father's great and glorious family? They had a *deep interest* in your salvation whilst they *remained* with you. Have they *lost* that interest *now?* Have they become in heaven so selfish and so careless about your salvation, that the tidings of your spiritual deliverance produce no emotion in their bosoms, even whilst the whole population of heaven are rejoicing over your repentance? It cannot be!

Finally, did you promise *one* or *all* of these, when you stood beside them in their death-chamber, and when you looked upon them breathing heavily upon their bed of dissolution, that you would *no longer* turn your back upon God, and trifle with your immortal interests, but that you would begin in real earnestness to live for Jehovah, and to spend your day of grace in seeking from God the salvation of your soul?

Surely you have not *forgotten* that promise, or *failed* to fulfil it? Oh! I earnestly entreat you, I beseech you by the mercy of God, by the grace of Jesus, by the compassion and love of the Holy Spirit, by the terrors and by the agonies of hell, by the glories and by the joys of heaven, and by the interest which you still have in these departed friends of yours who are now in heaven, remember your promise which you made to them before they left you. Remember it so as to act upon it even *now!* Arise in the strength of the Lord God Almighty! Return to your Father! Close with Him who is ready and willing to receive you into covenant with himself! Shake off at once and for ever the lethargies of your spiritual slumber!

Do this; and I tell you, that your return to God, the closing of your soul with Jesus by an act of appropriating faith, and by the transition of true repentance, will, even this *very moment*, send upwards a new thrill of joy into the bosoms of *your departed friends*, as well as into the bosoms of *all* who are in heaven; and the song of your spiritual espousals will now, even *now*, be sung, not only by your dear departed friends who have entered heaven before you, but by ten thousand times ten thousand, as they exultingly exclaim, "Let us be glad and rejoice, and give honor to Him; for the marriage of the Lamb is come, and another and another spiritual bride is making herself ready." Yes, reader, they are all ready to lift a special song of thanksgiving to God over thy repentance. "The Spirit and the bride say, Come; and let him that heareth say, Come; and let him that is athirst come; and whosoever will, let him take the water of life freely."

Heavenly-mindedness is one feature in the spiritual image of every believer. "Our conversation is in heaven; from whence also we look for the Saviour, the Lord Jesus Christ." "If ye, then, be risen with Christ, seek those things which are above, where Christ sitteth on the right hand of God." "Set your affection on things above." "But God, who is rich in mercy, for his great love wherewith he loved us, even when we were dead in sins, hath quickened us together with Christ (by grace ye are saved), and hath raised us up together, and made us sit together in heavenly places in Christ Jesus."

I am in the hope, that the views I have given in the preceding treatise may, by the blessing of God, lead Christians, by a prayerful perusal of them, to *lift their thoughts to heavenly things, and to converse about the home* which Jesus is preparing for them in the skies, and in which they are to *meet* and *spend their eternity* with the members of God's family who are there, in all the cordiality and in all the endearments of love and of friendship.

Again: I trust that I have succeeded to the satisfaction of my readers in *establishing the doctrine* of the *recognition of friends in heaven* as one of the *undoubted verities* of the Christian faith. I have viewed this doctrine of *future recognition*, not merely as a *problem* of abstract theological speculation, but as a *question*, that, if believed and entertained, *will* have a *great practical influence* upon the hearts and lives of all men. The *belief* that we are to *recognize our friends in heaven*, and *associate with them* for ever *there*, *with the full remembrance of the past*, throws the whole sublimity of eternity over our *present relationships* and *friendships*, and also over our Christian efforts to establish each other in the faith and in the divine life.

The belief that we are to *meet our friends* and *know* them in heaven *must* act as a *check* upon all *sinful actings* with them, and also as a *powerful motive* to *walk* with them *here* in the love and holiness, as far as possible, that distinguish the *communion of saints;* looking forward and looking upward to the time when we will *meet* and *walk with each other* through the heavens, and follow the Lamb whithersoever he goeth.

Further: I have set before you, my readers, the *interest* which *those* in *heaven* have in the *earth* and in *you*, as a *motive for action* in the ways of God. Have *all* who are in heaven, including, it may be, your departed *father* and *mother*, and *son* and *daughter*, and *brother* and *sister*, and *other* once dear, dear *friends*, this *deep* and *glowing* and *unquenchable* interest in *you* and in *your salvation?* Surely, then, it is not too much to expect that you should awaken, through this realization, to give heed to the things that belong to your peace, and to take *some* interest in your own spiritual emancipation.

Finally: I am in the hope, that the views I have given of *heaven as a home* may prove a *source* of *comfort* to your souls who are the people of God.

Are ye *poor?* Like Jesus once, have you not *a home* upon earth? Do not despond. Look up in hope. You have a *home* in yonder joyous *heaven*. Soon you will be in *it;* and the *remembrance* there of your present homeless wanderings and privations will make its rest and its riches appear, if possible, more delightful in your estimation.

Are ye in *bereavement?* Have you lost dear, yes, dearly and fondly beloved friends, who have fallen asleep in Jesus? Have you, in your present state of separation, the good hope, through grace, that they are *now* in *your* and in *their* Father's home? *Mourners in Zion!* your present separation from these once dear friends of yours is not for ever. *Soon* you will *meet* them *again* in *an eternal home of love*, and *recognize* them, and *speak* with them in the *language of heaven*, and *walk* with them in white through its courts of glory. *Oh! it will be to you the very bower of love to be with them again in the same home.*

Are you upon your *bed of dissolution?* Are you going the way of all the earth? What is *death* to *you*, believers? IT IS GOING HOME. God's home of glory is up *yonder! Its door of love is open! You are about to enter it! Yonder* you will *see* your *risen Lord*, and *meet your friends* in his *home of love*, and *be with them for ever!*

Boston: Printed by John Wilson and Son.

In Press,

BY THE AUTHOR OF "HEAVEN OUR HOME."

MEET FOR HEAVEN:

A STATE OF GRACE UPON EARTH

THE ONLY PREPARATION

FOR A STATE OF GLORY IN HEAVEN.

LIFE IN HEAVEN.

THERE FAITH IS CHANGED INTO SIGHT

AND

HOPE IS PASSED INTO BLISSFUL FRUITION.

ROBERTS BROTHERS, PUBLISHERS,

143, WASHINGTON STREET, BOSTON.

No. 143 WASHINGTON STREET,
Boston, October, 1863.

MESSRS. ROBERTS BROTHERS

LIST OF PUBLICATIONS.

POEMS. By JEAN INGELOW. In one volume. 16mo. Cloth, extra, $1.00.

"The new name undoubtedly belongs to a new poet, and this new volume will make the eyes of all lovers of poetry dance with a gladder light than if they had come upon a treasure-trove of gold. . . . Here is the unmistakable touch and breath of freshness; the clear early carol and dewy light. Here is the presence of Genius which cannot easily be defined, but which makes itself surely felt in a glow of delight such as makes the old world young again. Here is the power to fill common earthly facts with heavenly fire; a power to gladden wisely and to sadden nobly; to shake the heart, and bring moist tears into the eyes, through which the spirit may catch its loftiest light." — *London Athenæum.*

"It would be a great injustice to confound this volume with the mass of so-called poetry. . . . It contains something more than common-place thoughts clothed in tolerably pretty words. Nor is her volume, like too many of those of even the more tolerable verse-writers of the day, made up of a mass of comparative rubbish, relieved here and there by an isolated piece, to which it is not impossible conscientiously to award praise. One of the most striking characteristics of Miss Ingelow's poems is the remarkable evenness of their quality; and there is nothing in her volume which may not fairly claim to be regarded good. . . . Miss Ingelow's volume can scarcely fail to win for itself a warm welcome from all lovers of true poetry, and warrants us in anticipating that she will at some future time take a permanent place among English poets." — *London Spectator.*

HE POETRY OF THE EAST. By WILLIAM ROUNSEVILLE ALGER. In one volume. 12mo. Cloth, extra. Price 75 cents.

This is a complete Introduction to Oriental Poetry in all its families and departments; from the great epics of India, Persia, and Arabia, to their innumerable varieties of lyrical, descriptive, and aphoristic verse. It gives a critical account of the chief Eastern authors and their works, and illustrates them by hundreds of specimens. It is the only work of the kind in our language; and as such, no less than from its intrinsic merits, it possesses a unique value and charm.

"Its characterizations of the different branches of Eastern poetry are remarkably happy and accurate." — *H. H. Wilson, late President of the Royal Asiatic Society.*

"It is full of wisdom and beauty." — *John G. Whittier.*

"Extraordinary sentences for extraordinary readers." — *Ralph Waldo Emerson.*

"The modesty, enthusiasm, and interest of this book will keep it fresh and valuable." — *George William Curtis.*

"A golden volume, replete with sage thoughts and memorable sayings — a costly anthology, in which every specimen is either rich or strange." — *Frederick H. Hedge.*

"It will richly repay study to all who can find benefit in change of mental aliment, and who are willing to be led by a scholarly hand through the gorgeous and crowded Athenæum of Eastern literature." — *T. Starr King.*

"A masterpiece of Oriental scholarship."

"It reveals to our reading world *a new realm* of incomparable fascination."

OEMS. By CHARLES SWAIN. In one volume, with a fine portrait from a recent photograph, engraved by Smith. Blue and gold. Price $1.00.

This edition of Charles Swain's Poems embraces, in addition to the best poems in the different volumes published in England, several pieces which are now printed for the first time. There are upwards of three hundred songs, many of them so well known as to be almost "household words" throughout the land.

"Many of his songs have been wafted by their own ærial sweetness across the sea; and his felicitous description of Scott's funeral, (Dryburgh Abbey,) attended by a procession of the romancer's immortal characters, is too graphic a tribute to genius not to be recalled with delight." — *H. T. Tuckerman.*

BULWER LYTTON'S DRAMAS AND POEMS. In one volume, with a fine portrait on steel, by Schoff. Blue and gold. Price $1.00. Containing the Dramas of THE LADY OF LYONS, RICHELIEU, and MONEY, and Minor Poems.

"No living English writer is more read on the continent of Europe than Bulwer. His works have been translated into nearly all the living languages of Europe." — *New American Cyclopedia.*

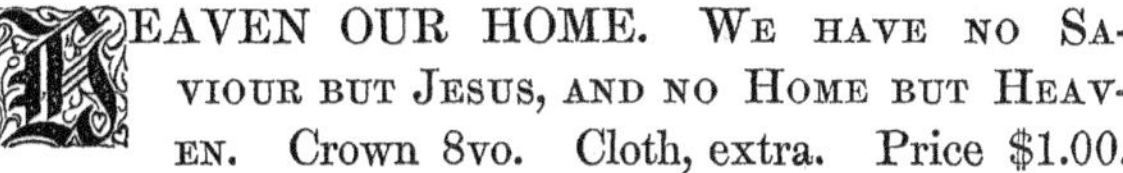

HEAVEN OUR HOME. WE HAVE NO SAVIOUR BUT JESUS, AND NO HOME BUT HEAVEN. Crown 8vo. Cloth, extra. Price $1.00.

OPINIONS OF THE ENGLISH PRESS.

"The author of the volume before us endeavors to describe what heaven is, as shown by the light of reason and Scripture; and we promise the reader many charming pictures of heavenly bliss, founded upon undeniable authority, and described with the pen of a dramatist, which cannot fail to elevate the soul as well as to delight the imagination. . . . . Part Second proves, in a manner as beautiful as it is convincing, the doctrine of the recognition of friends in heaven — a subject of which the author makes much, introducing many touching scenes of Scripture celebrities meeting in heaven and discoursing of their experience on earth. Part Third demonstrates the interest which those in heaven feel in earth, and proves with remarkable clearness that such an interest exists not only with the Almighty and among the angels, but also among the spirits of departed friends. We unhesitatingly give our opinion, that this volume is one of the most delightful productions of a religious character which has appeared for some time; and we would desire to see it pass into extensive circulation." — *Glasgow Herald.*

"This work gives positive and social views of heaven, as a counteraction to the negative and unsocial aspects in which the subject is so commonly presented." — *English Churchman.*

"Amid the works proceeding from an overteeming press, our attention has been arrested by the perusal of the above-named production, which, it seems, is wending its way daily among persons of all denominations. Certainly 'Heaven our Home,' whoever may be the author, is no common production." — *Airdrie Advertiser.*

"In boldness of conception, startling minuteness of delineation, and originality of illustration, this work, by an anonymous author, exceeds any of the kind we have ever read." — *John O' Groat Journal.*

"We are not in the least surprised at so many thousands of copies of this anonymous writer's being bought up. We seem to be listening to a voice and language which we never heard before. Matter comes at command; words flow with unstudied ease; the pages are full of life, light, and force; and the result is a stirring volume, which, while the Christian critic pronounces it free from affectation, even the man of taste, averse to evangelical religion, would admit it to be exempt from 'cant.'" — *London Patriot.*

"The name of the author of this work is strangely enough withheld. . . . . A social heaven, in which there will be the most perfect recognition, intercourse, fellowship, and bliss, is the leading idea of the book, and it is discussed in a fine genial spirit." — *Caledonian Mercury.*

IN PRESS.

MEET FOR HEAVEN. A STATE OF GRACE UPON EARTH THE ONLY PREPARATION FOR A STATE OF GLORY IN HEAVEN. By the Author of "Heaven our Home." Crown 8vo. Cloth, extra. Price $1.00.

OPINIONS OF THE ENGLISH PRESS.

"This forms a fitting companion to 'Heaven our Home,' — a volume which has been circulated by thousands, and which has found its way into almost every Christian family." — *Scottish Press.*

"What we shall be hereafter — whether our glorified souls will be like unto our souls here, or whether an entire change in their spiritual and moral condition will be effected after death — these are questions which occupy our thoughts, and to these the author has principally addressed himself." — *Cambridge University Chronicle.*

"The author, in his or her former work, 'Heaven our Home,' portrayed a Social Heaven, where scattered families meet at last in loving intercourse and in possession of perfect recognition, to spend a never-ending eternity of peace and love. In the present work the individual state of the children of God is attempted to be unfolded, and, more especially, the state of probation which is set apart for them on earth to fit and prepare erring mortals for the society of the saints. . . . .

"The work, as a whole, displays an originality of conception, a flow of language, and a closeness of reasoning rarely found in religious publications. . . . .

"The author combats the pleasing and generally-accepted belief that death will effect an entire change on the spiritual condition of our souls, and that all who enter into bliss will be placed on a common level." — *Glasgow Herald.*

"A careful perusal of this book will make it a less easy thing for a man to cheat himself into the notion that death will effect, not a mere transition and improvement, but an entire change in his moral and spiritual state. The dangerous nature of this delusion is exhibited with great power by the author of 'Meet for Heaven.'" — *Stirling Observer.*

"This, like the former volume, 'Heaven our Home,' by the same anonymous author, is a very remarkable book. Often as the subject has been handled, both by ancient and modern divines, it has never been touched with a bolder or a more masterly hand." — *John O' Groat Journal.*

IN PRESS.

LIFE IN HEAVEN. There, Faith is changed into Sight, and Hope is passed into Blissful Fruition. A New Work by the Author of "Heaven our Home," and "Meet for Heaven." Crown 8vo. Cloth, extra. Price $1.00.

This new work is a companion volume to "Heaven our Home," and "Meet for Heaven," and embraces a subject of very great interest, which has not been included in these volumes.

The two works above mentioned have already attained in England the large sale of 100,000 copies.

REV. J. H. INGRAHAM'S POPULAR WORKS.

THE PRINCE OF THE HOUSE OF DAVID; or, THREE YEARS IN THE HOLY CITY. Being a series of Letters of Adina, a Jewess of Alexandria, supposed to be sojourning in Jerusalem in the days of Herod, addressed to her father, a wealthy Jew in Egypt, and relating, as if by an eye-witness, all the scenes and wonderful incidents in the Life of Jesus of Nazareth, from his baptism in Jordan to his crucifixion on Calvary. By Rev. J. H. INGRAHAM. One volume. 12mo. Cloth, gilt. Price $1.50.

THE PILLAR OF FIRE; or, ISRAEL IN BONDAGE. Being an account of the wonderful scenes in the life of the Son of Pharaoh's Daughter, (Moses,) together with picturesque sketches of the Hebrews under their Taskmasters. By Rev. J. H. INGRAHAM. One volume. 12mo. Cloth, gilt. Price $1.50.

THE THRONE OF DAVID, FROM THE CONSECRATION OF THE SHEPHERD OF BETHLEHEM TO THE REBELLION OF PRINCE ABSALOM. Being an illustration of the splendor, power, and dominion of the reign of the Shepherd — Poet — Warrior — King and Prophet — Ancestor and Type of Jesus; in a series of letters addressed by an Assyrian Ambassador, to his lord and king on the throne of Nineveh. By Rev. J. H. INGRAHAM. One volume. 12mo. Cloth, gilt. Price $1.50.

JUVENILES.

THE HISTORY OF SANDFORD AND MERTON. By THOMAS DAY, Esq. A new edition; revised throughout, and embellished with very numerous engravings. One volume. Square 16mo. Fancy cloth, gilt. Price $1.25.

POPULAR FAIRY TALES; containing the choicest and best known Fairy Stories. Illustrated by engravings from designs by the most celebrated French artists. First and second series. Square 16mo. Fancy cloth, gilt. Price of each series, (sold separately,) $1.00.

PAUL PRESTON'S VOYAGES, TRAVELS, AND REMARKABLE ADVENTURES, as related by himself. With numerous illustrations. Square 16mo. Fancy cloth, gilt. Price $1.00.

THE FAIRY LIBRARY, containing —

Popular Fairy Tales — First Series;
" " " — Second Series;
Paul Preston's Adventures.

Illustrated. Three volumes, in a neat box. Fancy cloth, gilt. Price $3.00.

FABLES AND NURSERY READINGS, containing Eighteen approved Nursery Fables, interspersed with readings for the nursery. Fully illustrated. Square 16mo. Fancy cloth, gilt. Price 63 cents.

SIMPLE LESSONS FOR LITTLE LEARNERS, on a popular plan. Part First, words of one and two syllables. Part Second, words of more than two syllables. To which is added, COBWEBS TO CATCH FLIES; or, Dialogues in short sentences, adapted to children from the age of three to eight years. With characteristic illustrations. One volume. Square 16mo. Fancy cloth, gilt. Price 63 cents.

FAREWELL TALES. By Mrs. Hofland, author of the "Merchant's Widow," &c. With engravings. One volume. Square 16mo. Fancy cloth, gilt. Price 63 cents.

THE LITTLE LEARNER'S LIBRARY, containing — Simple Lessons for Little Learners;
Fables and Nursery Readings;
Mrs. Hofland's Farewell Tales.

Illustrated. Three volumes, in a neat box. Fancy cloth, gilt. Price $1.88.

FIRESIDE TALES, in Prose and Verse. By Mary Howitt. With illustrations. One volume. 16mo. Fancy cloth, gilt. Price 75 cents.

THE SCOTTISH ORPHANS; a Moral Tale, founded on an historical fact; to which is added, Arthur Monteith, a continuation of the Scottish Orphans. By Mrs. Blackford. One volume. 16mo. Fancy cloth, gilt. Price 63 cents.

THE FIRESIDE LIBRARY, containing —
Fireside Tales. By Mary Howitt;
The Turtle Dove; and other Stories. By Mary Howitt;
The Christmas Tree, and other Stories. By Mary Howitt;
The Scottish Orphans; a Moral Tale. By Mrs. Blackford;
Arthur Monteith; a sequel to the Scottish Orphans. By Mrs. Blackford;
Helen and her Cousins; or, Two Months at Ashfield Rectory.

Illustrated. Six volumes, with a neat box. 16mo. Fancy cloth, gilt. Price $2.25.

www.ingramcontent.com/pod-product-compliance
Lightning Source LLC
LaVergne TN
LVHW020224110826
845151LV00003B/821

* 9 7 8 1 4 2 5 5 3 2 2 3 9 *